GORDON RAMSAY

D0551775

MAKES IT
easy

GORDON RAMSAY

with Mark Sargeant and Helen Tillott
photographs by Jill Mead

MAKES IT
easy

Quadrille

contents

Publishing consultant Anne Furniss
Art director Helen Lewis
Project editor Janet Illsley
Photographer Jill Mead
Food stylist Mark Sargeant
Home economist Helen Tillott
Production Vincent Smith

This paperback edition first published in 2006 by
Quadrille Publishing Limited, Alhambra House
27–31 Charing Cross Road, London WC2H 0LS

10 9 8 7 6 5 4 3

Text © 2005 Gordon Ramsay
Photography © 2005 Jill Mead
Design and layout © 2005 Quadrille Publishing Limited

Cataloguing in Publication Data: a catalogue record for this
book is available from the British Library.

ISBN-13: 978 184400 324 2
ISBN-10: 1 84400 324 8
Printed in China

notes

All spoon measures are level unless otherwise stated:
1 tsp = 5ml spoon; 1 tbsp = 15 ml spoon.

All herbs are fresh and all pepper is freshly ground black pepper.

Egg sizes are specified where they are critical, otherwise use large eggs.
I recommend free-range eggs. If you are pregnant or in a vulnerable health group,
avoid those recipes that contain raw egg whites or lightly cooked eggs.

My oven timings are for fan-assisted ovens. If you are using a conventional
oven increase the temperature by 10°C (½ Gas Mark). Individual ovens can deviate
by as much as 10°C from the setting, either way. Get to know your oven and use
an oven thermometer to check its accuracy. My timings are provided as guidelines,
with a description of colour or texture where appropriate.

introduction

Cooking still excites and entices me, just as it did when I opened the doors of my first restaurant in 1993. Food is constantly evolving and I love the challenge of creating new dishes for my customers. However, I am not a fan of trendy, contrived food – it doesn't satisfy me. I would far rather eat a tasty homemade fish pie than a tower of fish smothered with an unidentifiable sauce. The quality of ingredients is paramount to the success of a dish and I always source foods from top quality producers. With every dish, I strive to achieve a balance of flavours, enhancing the individual tastes and textures of ingredients without masking or overpowering any of them.

Cooking with Tana and the family has opened up a whole new area for me. Above all, food is to be enjoyed, with family, friends and loved ones – but in our busy lives time for cooking is often limited. The solution is to choose dishes that taste great, are made from the best ingredients, but are simple in their execution. In this book, I hope to inspire you by using my experience to make things easy. Cooking and eating fabulous food together – whether it's a family meal, a barbecue with friends or a romantic dinner for two – is fun and rewarding. Enjoy…

breakfast
and brunch

There's nothing quite like a proper breakfast to start the day. I love a traditional English breakfast, and not necessarily first thing. A mid-morning brunch is essential fuel in the restaurants to get the brigade through lunch service. Easy nutritious food is what's needed and it's much the same at home. I encourage the family to vary their breakfasts, and make the most of seasonal fruit – a fresh cherry compote is popular in summer. My spiced breakfast bread is worth a try too – as an alternative to croissants or toast.

country garden breakfast

Serves 4

200g new potatoes

sea salt and pepper

4 large flat field
    mushrooms, trimmed

4 large English tomatoes,
    halved

1 tbsp butter, plus extra to
    grease

4 free-range eggs

4 tbsp double cream

1 tbsp olive oil

Heat the oven to 200°C/Gas 6. Boil the new potatoes in salted water until just tender, then drain well and crush slightly.

Put the mushrooms and tomatoes in a large non-stick sauté pan, dot with the butter and season with pepper. Cover and leave to cook gently until softened.

Butter 4 ramekins, break an egg into each one and pour on the cream. Season with pepper and bake for 5–7 minutes.

Meanwhile, heat the olive oil in a small frying pan until hot but not smoking, add the potatoes and fry until golden brown and crispy.

Serve the baked egg ramekins on warm plates with the mushrooms, tomatoes and crispy potatoes.

salmon kedgeree

Serves 4

375g filleted salmon, skinned

1 tsp turmeric

225g basmati rice, rinsed

pinch of saffron threads

4 tbsp olive oil

100g cherry tomatoes, halved

4 free-range eggs

400ml fish stock (approximately)

2 spring onions or shallots, chopped

75g unsalted butter, in pieces

3 tbsp chopped flat-leaf parsley

sea salt and pepper

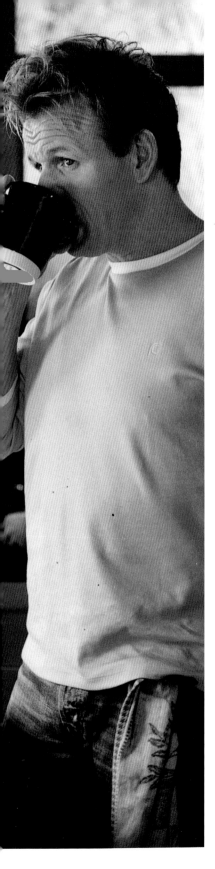

Cut the salmon into chunks, sprinkle with the turmeric and set aside to marinate.

Put the rice in a pan with 500ml cold water, bring to the boil and simmer for 7–8 minutes until the liquid is absorbed. Tip into a shallow bowl, sprinkle with the saffron and leave to stand.

Heat 2 tbsp olive oil in a frying pan and cook the salmon chunks for about 1 minute on each side. Remove and drain on kitchen paper.

Add the tomatoes to the pan with another 1 tbsp olive oil and cook, stirring, for 1 minute. Remove and set aside.

Boil the eggs for 6–8 minutes, then peel, halve and set aside. Bring the fish stock to the boil in a pan and keep at a low simmer.

Heat the remaining oil in a medium pan and cook the onions for 2–3 minutes to soften. Add a third of the butter, then the blanched rice and cook, stirring, to coat in the butter.

Add a ladleful of hot stock and stir until the liquid is absorbed. Continue to add the stock, a ladleful at a time, stirring over the heat, until the rice is cooked. Add the remaining butter and stir until melted.

Fork the salmon through the rice. Add the tomatoes, parsley and salt to taste, and heat through gently. Pile on to warm plates, add the halved boiled eggs and grind over some pepper. Serve immediately.

salmon kedgeree

"I like to eat my scrambled eggs topped with pan-fried mushrooms and cherry tomatoes on the vine"

sublime scrambled eggs
ON TOAST

Serves 2–3

6 large free-range eggs

25g ice-cold butter, cut into small dice

1 tbsp crème fraîche

sea salt and pepper

few chives, snipped

To serve:

2–3 chunky slices of rustic bread, such as pain Polaîne

Break the eggs into a cold, heavy-based pan, place on the lowest heat possible and add half the butter. Using a spatula, stir the eggs frequently to combine the yolks with the whites.

As the mixture begins to set, add the remaining butter. The eggs will take about 4–5 minutes to scramble – they should still be soft and quite lumpy. Don't let them get too hot – keep moving the pan off and back on the heat.

Toast the bread slices on both sides in the meantime.

Add the crème fraîche and season the eggs at the last minute, then add the snipped chives. Put the toast on warm plates, pile the softly scrambled eggs on top and serve immediately.

bubble and squeak
WITH SMOKED HADDOCK

Serves 4

550g Desirée potatoes, peeled

sea salt and pepper

500ml milk

300g smoked haddock fillet

180g Savoy cabbage, cored and finely chopped

1 onion, finely chopped

3 tbsp vegetable oil

25g butter

Boil the potatoes in salted water until soft, then drain and press through a potato ricer into a large bowl (or mash well). Put to one side.

Bring the milk to the boil in a small frying pan and poach the smoked haddock for 3–4 minutes. Take off the heat and allow to cool in the liquid.

Blanch the cabbage in boiling salted water for 2–3 minutes, then drain and refresh in cold water.

Sauté the onion in 1 tbsp oil until soft. Add to the potato with the butter and cabbage, mix well and season generously. Drain the haddock, flake and fold into the potato mixture.

Heat the remaining oil in a non-stick medium frying pan. Add the potato mixture and press down with the back of a spoon to form a 'cake'. Cook for 10 minutes until the base is golden brown.

Turn on to a plate, then slide the potato cake back into the pan and cook for a further 5–7 minutes. Serve immediately.

English breakfast

Serves 4

3 tbsp vegetable oil, plus
  extra to fry eggs
4 or 8 good-quality butcher's
  pork sausages
4 slices black pudding
8 smoked back bacon
  rashers
4 slices good, thick sliced
  bread
4 large flat or field
  mushrooms, trimmed
1 bunch vine-ripened cherry
  tomatoes, stalks removed
sea salt and pepper
4 free-range eggs (ideally
  duck's eggs)

Heat the oven to 120°C/Gas $^1/_2$ and put 4 dinner plates and a large platter inside to warm.

Heat 3 tbsp oil in a large, heavy-based frying pan. Add the sausages and black pudding, and cook slowly for 6–8 minutes to release the fat. Turn up the heat, add the bacon and cook until it begins to crisp and the sausages are brown. Transfer to the warmed platter in the oven.

Heat the fat left in the pan until you can see a haze (adding a little more oil if needed). Add the bread and fry quickly on one side until golden brown. Remove and drain on kitchen paper, then add to the platter in the oven.

Lower the heat and add the mushrooms and tomatoes to the frying pan. Season with pepper, cover and cook for 5 minutes.

Meanwhile, heat a little oil in a small frying pan. Break an egg into a breakfast cup and carefully tip into the hot pan. Repeat with the other eggs (if fresh they will 'sit up' and not spread all over the pan). Cook until the white is completely set and firm.

Immediately transfer a fried egg to each warm plate and season with salt and pepper. Add the sausages, black pudding, bacon, fried bread, tomatoes and mushrooms. Serve at once.

English
breakfast

spiced breakfast bread

Makes 10–12 slices

butter to grease
3 free-range eggs
50g light brown sugar
250g thin honey
125ml milk
125g plain flour
125g buckwheat flour
1 tsp five-spice powder
1 tbsp ground mixed spice
2 tbsp baking powder
finely grated zest of
  2 oranges

Heat the oven to 160°C/Gas 3. Lightly butter a 25x10cm loaf tin.

Whisk the eggs and sugar together in a large bowl over a pan of hot water, using an electric whisk, until the mixture is pale and thickened (enough to leave a ribbon when the beaters are lifted). Remove the pan from the heat, but leave the bowl set over it.

Warm the honey and milk together in a small pan and gradually beat into the egg mixture until evenly mixed.

Sift the flours, spices and baking powder together into a large mixing bowl and carefully fold in the egg mixture, followed by the orange zest.

Spoon the mixture into the loaf tin and bake for 35–40 minutes until well risen, firm to the touch and golden brown on top. Leave in the tin for 5 minutes, then turn out and cool on a wire rack.

Serve warm, cut into slices. Best eaten on the day it is made (any leftover can be frozen). Delicious with a compote of cherries (see overleaf).

toasted bagel

WITH SERRANO HAM AND GRILLED
TOMATOES

" I love New York and the fresh hot bagel stalls on every other corner – perfect for a breakfast on the move. Smoked salmon and cream cheese may be the traditional filling but there's really no limit. I also like smoked chicken with rocket, and egg mayonnaise with grilled maple bacon"

Serves 4

4 bagels
4 large vine-ripened beef tomatoes
pepper
a little olive oil to brush
8 slices Serrano ham

Heat the grill to high. Split the bagels in half.

Cut the tomatoes into 5mm slices, place on a baking tray and season with pepper. Brush with olive oil and cook under the grill for a few minutes to soften. Remove the tray from the grill.

Toast the split bagels under the grill until crisp and golden brown on both sides.

Put the bagel bases on warm plates, pile the grilled tomato slices on top and cover with the Serrano ham slices. Sandwich together with the bagel tops and serve.

"We are so lucky to have such fabulous fruit in this country, why we ship vast quantities in from abroad rather than make the most of seasonal produce is beyond me. Sampling the different cherry varieties in a beautiful Kent orchard last autumn inspired me to create this simple recipe"

compote of cherries

Serves 6

1kg mixed fresh cherries
250ml fresh orange juice
100g sugar
pared zest of 1 lemon
few mint leaves

Pit the cherries and put into a stainless steel or non-reactive saucepan with the orange juice, sugar, lemon zest and mint leaves. Slowly bring to the boil and then simmer for 5 minutes, shaking the pan occasionally to prevent the cherries sticking.

Tip into a bowl and allow to cool, then remove the mint leaves and lemon zest. Cover and keep in the fridge until needed (up to 3 days), but bring back to room temperature to serve.

Serve the compote with Greek-style yogurt.

banana and passion fruit smoothie

Serves 4

4 bananas (in skins)
4 passion fruit, halved
400ml chilled natural yogurt
100ml chilled milk
2 tsp thin honey

Put the bananas in the freezer for an hour or two. (The skins will blacken, but that's fine.)

Scoop out the passion fruit pulp and press through a sieve into a blender. Peel the bananas and add to the blender with the yogurt, milk and honey. Whiz until smooth, pour into glasses and serve.

great
fast food

Fast food is now synonymous with ready-meals and take-aways, which is a sad state of affairs. So many fresh foods are incredibly quick to prepare and easily assembled into tempting fast meals – such as soups, omelettes, warm salads and pasta dishes. Keeping a well-stocked storecupboard is the key to great fast food. You will be amazed just how quick these recipes are to prepare. In the time it takes to reheat a ready-meal, you can put a homemade soup, smart pasta dish, or a creamy risotto on the table.

broccoli soup

Serves 4

1kg broccoli

sea salt and pepper

4 slices soft goat's cheese,
 or 4 baby chèvres

50g flaked almonds or
 walnuts, lightly toasted

extra virgin olive oil to drizzle

Cut the broccoli into florets. Bring 800ml salted water to the boil in a pan, add the broccoli and simmer for about 4 minutes until tender but still bright green. Drain, reserving the liquid.

Whiz the broccoli in a blender, with enough of the liquid to half-fill the goblet, to give a velvety texture.

Reheat the soup in the pan; adjust the seasoning. Put the goat's cheese slices into warm soup bowls and pour in the soup, to one side. Top with the nuts, grind over some pepper and drizzle with olive oil to serve.

seared scallops and lettuce
ON RUSTIC BREAD

Serves 4

olive oil to brush

16 medium to large scallops,
   shelled and cleaned

4 large slices rustic bread

butter to spread

2 Little Gem lettuces,
   separated into leaves

squeeze of lemon juice

extra virgin olive oil to drizzle

sea salt and pepper

lemon wedges to serve

Heat a griddle pan and brush with a little olive oil. When very hot, place the scallops on the griddle and cook for 2 minutes, then turn and cook for a further $1-1^1/_2$ minutes – no longer or they will toughen.

Meanwhile, toast the bread on both sides until golden. Butter very lightly, while still warm. Put a slice on each plate.

Pile the lettuce on to the toasted bread and tuck the griddled scallops between the leaves. Squeeze a little lemon juice over the scallops and drizzle with a little extra virgin olive oil. Season well with salt and pepper and serve, with lemon wedges.

"I admire the traditional baker. Having done two stints as a night baker, I appreciate the care that goes into each and every loaf. There are plenty of good bakeries producing excellent rustic bread, so find your nearest one and avoid synthetic white bread at all costs"

"This is a great way to use up leftover roast pork belly (see page 80); you can also buy crispy roast pork from Chinatown and some good deli counters"

sandwich of crispy pork
WITH SOURDOUGH BREAD

Serves 4

1 tbsp olive oil, plus extra to
  brush
1 large red onion, finely sliced
1 garlic clove, finely chopped
8 thick slices sourdough bread
1 Little Gem lettuce, separated
  into leaves
4 slices roast pork belly
sea salt and pepper

Heat the olive oil in a heavy-based pan and sauté the onion and garlic over a low heat for 5–7 minutes to soften, without browning.

Lightly toast the bread on both sides. Put a slice on each of 4 plates. Brush lightly with olive oil and arrange the lettuce leaves on top.

Lay the pork slices on the lettuce and top with the sautéed onion. Season with salt and pepper. Sandwich together with the other toasted bread slices, cut in half and serve.

tortilla wrap
WITH CHICKEN AND AVOCADO

Serves 4

3–4 free-range boneless chicken breasts

3 tbsp olive oil

juice of 1 lime

1 tsp ground cumin

1 tsp ground coriander

1 onion, roughly chopped

1 red pepper, deseeded and roughly chopped

6 vine-ripened tomatoes, cut into quarters

8 tortilla wraps

1 tbsp chopped coriander leaves

2 avocados

125ml Greek-style yogurt

"Wraps are a convenient fast food option. As an alternative to chicken, use monkfish or salmon fillet, cut into medallions"

Cut the chicken into thin strips. Combine the olive oil, lime juice and spices in a bowl. Add the chicken, toss to mix and leave to marinate for 2 hours. Heat the oven to 200°C/Gas 6.

Heat a heavy-based frying pan or griddle until very hot. Add the chicken in its marinade, with the onion, red pepper and half the tomatoes. Cook for 4–5 minutes.

Wrap the tortillas in foil and warm in the oven for 5 minutes. Add the rest of the tomatoes to the frying pan and cook for a further 2 minutes. Scatter over the chopped coriander.

Halve, peel and thinly slice the avocados, discarding the stones. Divide the chicken mixture between the warm tortillas, add a few avocado slices and a dollop of yogurt to each one, then roll up. Serve two per person.

grilled fresh sardines

WITH A NEW POTATO AND CRÈME FRAÎCHE SALAD

Serves 4

12 new potatoes, such as Charlotte

sea salt and pepper

4 tbsp crème fraîche

1 tbsp lemon juice

2 tsp snipped chives, plus extra to garnish

8 small fresh sardines, cleaned, boned and butterflied

olive oil, to oil

1 Little Gem lettuce, separated into leaves

a little classic vinaigrette

lemon wedges to serve

Boil the new potatoes in their skins in salted water until tender. Drain, tip into a bowl and lightly crush with the back of a fork, then allow to cool. Add the crème fraîche, lemon juice and snipped chives, and season well with salt and pepper.

Heat the grill to maximum. Lay the sardines, skin-side up, in an oiled baking tray and grill for 3–4 minutes. Turn them over and cook for a further 2–3 minutes. Remove from the grill and season well.

Place a few lettuce leaves on each plate and pile the potato salad on top. Arrange the hot sardines, skin-side up, on the salad. Drizzle with a little vinaigrette and serve immediately, topped with a few chives and accompanied by lemon wedges.

open omelette

OF SMOKED SALMON AND CRÈME FRAÎCHE

Serves 4

6 free-range eggs

sea salt and pepper

1 tbsp olive oil

25g butter

200g smoked salmon, cut
    into strips

100ml crème fraîche

small bunch of chives,
    snipped

Heat the grill to high. Break the eggs into a bowl, whisk with a fork and season with pepper.

Heat the olive oil in a cast-iron frying pan, add the butter and allow to melt. Increase the heat to medium-high and, when the pan is hot, pour in the egg mixture. Leave until the eggs start to set, then with a metal spatula, draw the edge of the mixture towards the centre of the pan.

Cook for 30 seconds or so until the base of the omelette is set (the top will appear quite wet), then put the pan under the grill for 30 seconds or until the omelette is lightly set on top but not dry. Remove from the heat.

Scatter the smoked salmon on top of the omelette and dot with the crème fraîche. Sprinkle with the snipped chives and season with salt and pepper to taste. Loosen the edges, then slide the omelette out of the pan. Cut into wedges and serve immediately.

"If girolles are out of season and other wild mushrooms are hard to find, use a mixture of chestnut and oyster mushrooms"

risotto of wild mushrooms

Serves 4

750ml vegetable stock

3 tbsp olive oil

2 large shallots, finely diced

2 celery sticks, finely sliced

200g risotto rice

1 small glass dry white wine

1 tsp ground coriander
  seeds

sea salt and pepper

100g oyster mushrooms,
  cleaned and sliced

100g girolles, ceps or other
  wild mushrooms, cleaned
  and sliced

2 tbsp mascarpone or
  crème fraîche

1 tbsp chopped chervil or
  chives

2 tbsp freshly grated
  Parmesan

Bring the stock to the boil in a pan and keep it at a low simmer.

Heat 1 tbsp olive oil in a deep sauté pan, add the shallots and sauté for 2–3 minutes until softened but not coloured. Add the celery and cook for a further 2 minutes.

Stir in the rice and cook for 2 minutes. Pour in the wine and cook until it has been absorbed, then add a ladleful of the hot stock with the ground coriander and cook, stirring, until the liquid has been absorbed.

Continue to add the stock a ladleful at a time, allowing each addition to be absorbed before adding any more, until the rice is al dente (cooked but firm to the bite). The risotto should be very moist and creamy. Season with salt and pepper to taste.

Heat the remaining olive oil in a sauté pan, add the sliced mushrooms and cook, stirring frequently, until softened, then stir through the risotto.

Add the mascarpone or crème fraîche, stir and divide the risotto between warm plates. Scatter the herbs and Parmesan over and serve.

risotto of wild mushrooms

butternut squash puff 'pizza'
WITH SAGE AND SMOKED CHEDDAR

Serves 4

2 tbsp olive oil

450g chopped butternut
squash

330g ready-made puff
pastry

1 egg yolk beaten with 1 tsp
water (eggwash)

200g smoked Cheddar
cheese, grated

4 sage leaves, finely
chopped, plus extra to
garnish

sea salt and pepper

Heat the oven to 220°C/Gas 7. Heat the olive oil in a
pan, add the squash and sweat gently for 5 minutes.

Roll out the pastry to a large rectangle, about
15x25cm. Using a sharp knife, mark a 1cm border
around the edge of the pastry, without cutting right
through. Brush the border with eggwash.

Sprinkle half the cheese on the pastry within the
border and top with the squash. Scatter the chopped
sage over and season with salt and pepper.

Bake for 20 minutes, then scatter over the
remaining cheese and cook for a further 5 minutes.
Garnish with fresh sage leaves and serve.

salad of smoked eel
WITH BACON AND SAUTÉ POTATOES

Serves 4

12 new potatoes, such as La Ratte, cleaned

sea salt and pepper

2–3 tbsp olive oil

50g bacon lardons

300g smoked eel fillets

3 tbsp classic vinaigrette

2 Little Gem lettuce, separated into leaves

herby mascarpone (optional, see right)

"I sometimes serve this salad topped with a spoonful of herby mascarpone. Simply stir some chopped herbs (such as chervil, parsley and dill) salt, pepper and a squeeze of lemon juice into some mascarpone"

Par-boil the potatoes in salted water for 7–8 minutes until barely tender, then drain. Allow to cool, then halve lengthways.

Heat the olive oil in a frying pan. Add the potatoes, cut-side down, and cook quickly over a high heat until golden brown, adding a little more oil if needed. Drain on kitchen paper.

Remove excess oil from the pan with kitchen paper, then add the bacon lardons and cook over a high heat until crisp. Drain on kitchen paper.

Cut the eel fillets into strips and warm through gently in a small pan with 2 tbsp of the vinaigrette. Toss the lettuce leaves with the remaining vinaigrette.

Divide the lettuce between plates, scatter over the lardons and place the warm potatoes on top. Spoon the warm flaked eel in the centre and top with a dollop of herby mascarpone if you like.

spaghetti with lobster
IN A CREAMY TOMATO SAUCE

Serves 4

1 freshly cooked lobster,
   about 1kg
600g cherry tomatoes, diced
2–3 spring onions, finely
   sliced or shredded
1 chilli, deseeded and
   chopped
1 garlic clove, chopped
50g unsalted butter
sea salt and pepper
1 glass dry white wine
500g fresh spaghetti
1 tbsp olive oil
100ml double cream
handful of basil leaves,
   chopped
freshly shaved Parmesan
   to serve
olive oil to drizzle

To extract the lobster meat, cut through the body shell and take out the meat in one piece, pulling out the dirt sac from the third disc. Extract the meat from the claws by cracking the shells open with the back of a knife or a nutcracker. Chop the body and claw meat into bite-sized pieces; set aside.

Put the cherry tomatoes, spring onions, chilli, garlic and butter in a heavy-based pan and cook over a medium heat until soft but not coloured. Season with pepper, add the wine and cook until it has evaporated.

Add the spaghetti to a large pan of boiling salted water with the olive oil and cook until al dente (tender but firm to the bite), about 3 minutes.

Meanwhile, add the lobster to the sauce and stir in the cream and chopped basil. Warm through gently for a couple of minutes.

Drain the pasta and toss with the lobster sauce. Divide between warm plates, scatter the Parmesan over and drizzle with a little olive oil. Serve immediately.

"I love this incongruous combination of lobster – the king of shellfish – with simple spaghetti and fresh tomato. It's a great fast pasta dish for a special occasion"

macaroni cheese

WITH BEENLEIGH BLUE AND MUSHROOMS

Serves 4

250g dried macaroni

sea salt and pepper

1 tbsp olive oil

50g butter

100g ceps or chestnut mushrooms, sliced

200ml double cream

100g Beenleigh blue cheese

Add the macaroni to a large pan of boiling salted water with the olive oil and cook for 7–10 minutes until just tender. Drain and rinse under cold water to remove excess starch. Return to the pan and set aside.

Melt the butter in a small frying pan. Add the mushrooms and fry until softened and golden brown, then season with pepper. Heat the grill.

Add the cream to the macaroni and crumble in two-thirds of the blue cheese. Heat gently for a few minutes to melt the cheese. Season with pepper.

Transfer the macaroni cheese to a gratin dish and scatter on the mushrooms and remaining cheese. Place under the hot grill for 2–3 minutes to brown lightly, then serve.

"I recommend you always buy free-range organic chicken – the flavour is far superior to that of intensively reared birds fed on a limited diet with minimal exercise"

warm chicken salad
WITH JERUSALEM ARTICHOKES, SPINACH AND BACON

Serves 4

2 rosemary sprigs

3 thyme sprigs

1 bay leaf

2 garlic cloves, peeled

500ml chicken stock

2–3 free-range chicken
   breasts (part-boned)

4 tbsp olive oil

50g butter

150g Jerusalem artichokes,
   scrubbed or peeled

2 tbsp lemon juice

125g bacon rashers

50ml classic vinaigrette

1 tsp sherry vinegar

1 shallot, finely chopped

150g baby spinach

deep-fried onion rings to
   serve (optional)

Put the herbs, garlic and stock in a pan and bring to a simmer. Add the chicken breasts and poach gently for 3 minutes or until firm to touch. Cool in the liquor, then lift out and remove from the bone, keeping the skin intact.

Fry the chicken breasts, skin-side down, in half the olive oil for 4–5 minutes until the skin is golden brown and crisp. Add half the butter and cook for another 2 minutes.

Simmer the artichokes in water to cover, with the lemon juice added, for 5–6 minutes. Drain, cool and thickly slice. Fry the artichoke slices in the remaining oil and butter for 2–3 minutes each side until golden brown. Drain on kitchen paper. Pan-fry the bacon until crisp, drain and cut into pieces.

Whisk the vinaigrette with the sherry vinegar and shallot. Cut each chicken breast lengthways into 6 slices. Arrange the spinach, chicken, bacon and artichokes on plates and dress with the vinaigrette. Garnish with fried onion rings if you like and serve.

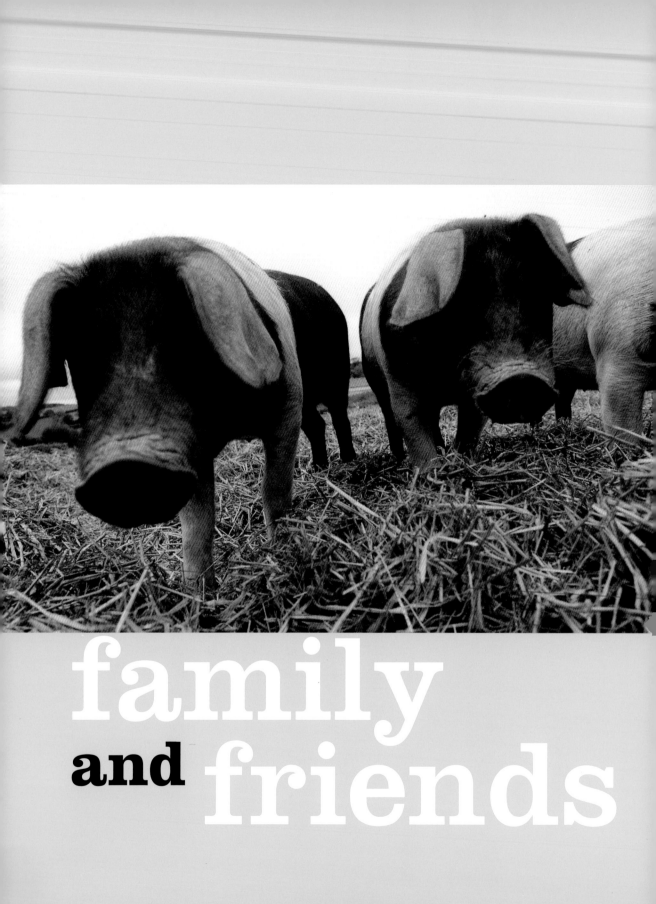

family and friends

Eating together as a family is important to me. My mother always made us sit down together to eat and I have fond memories of the food, as well as the laughter. Sunday is our family day and we often have a roast, but I also like to cook meals that are easy to prepare and serve. We never quite know how many of us there will be, so meals need to be flexible. My fish pie is a favourite, but the children also enjoy braised beef or a chicken casserole. Desserts are a must and we never tire of steamed pudding or trifle.

roasted cod and tomatoes
WITH OVEN CHIPS

Serves 4

700g Maris Piper potatoes

2 tbsp olive oil

25g butter

675g cod loin fillet, skinned
   and cut into 4 thick pieces

12 cherry tomatoes on the
   vine, cut into 4 clusters

juice of ½ lemon

sea salt and pepper

2 tbsp chopped parsley

Heat the oven to 200°C/Gas 6. Peel the potatoes and cut into chunky chips. Add to a pan of boiling water and blanch for 4 minutes; drain well. Return to the dry pan, add the olive oil and shake the pan to coat the chips in the oil. Spread the chips out on a baking tray and bake for 10 minutes. Shake the tray to turn the chips and bake for a further 10–15 minutes.

Meanwhile, melt the butter in a cast-iron frying pan, add the fish and cook for 2–3 minutes. Turn and cook the other side for 2 minutes, then add the tomatoes to the pan and place in the oven. (If your pan isn't ovenproof, simply transfer to an oiled roasting pan.) Bake for 5 minutes.

Drizzle the lemon juice over the fish as you take it from the oven. Season with salt and pepper and then allow to rest in the pan for 5 minutes. Put the cooked chips into a warm bowl and season with salt.

Place the roasted cod and tomatoes on warm plates, scatter the parsley over and drizzle with the pan juices. Serve at once, with the oven chips.

fillets of red mullet
WITH A RUSTIC RATATOUILLE

Serves 4

4 small red mullet about 250g each, or
   2 larger ones about 500g each, filleted

2 tbsp olive oil

sea salt and pepper

Rustic ratatouille:

2 beef tomatoes

$\frac{1}{2}$ red pepper, deseeded

$\frac{1}{2}$ yellow pepper, deseeded

1 tbsp olive oil

2 garlic cloves, finely chopped

1 red onion, finely chopped

2 courgettes, chopped

1 aubergine, chopped

handful of basil leaves, roughly chopped

dash of balsamic vinegar

For the ratatouille, halve and deseed the tomatoes, then finely chop the flesh. Cut the peppers into 1cm dice. Heat the olive oil in a saucepan and cook the garlic and onion gently for 2 minutes to soften. Add the courgettes, aubergine and tomatoes, stir and cook for about 5 minutes to soften. Add the basil, balsamic vinegar and seasoning to taste. Take off the heat and keep warm.

To cook the red mullet, heat the olive oil in a heavy-based frying pan, then add the red mullet fillets, skin-side down, and cook for about 3 minutes until the skin is really crispy. Turn and cook for a further 30 seconds–1 minute, depending on the thickness of the fish. Remove from the heat, season with salt and pepper and leave to rest for a few minutes.

Spoon the ratatouille on to warm plates or a large platter. Top with the red mullet fillets and serve.

fillets of red mullet

gordon's fish pie

Serves 4

25g butter

4 shallots, finely chopped

250ml dry white wine

250ml Noilly Prat or dry
  vermouth

500ml fish stock

500ml double cream

sea salt and pepper

800g mixed white filleted
  fish (cod, haddock,
  monkfish etc)

juice of ½ lemon

handful of tarragon, flat-leaf
  parsley or chervil, chopped

300g ready-made puff
  pastry

1 egg yolk, beaten with
  1 tsp water (eggwash)

Heat the butter in a pan and sweat the shallots until soft. Add the wine and vermouth and let bubble until reduced by half. Add the stock and reduce again by half.

Add the cream and boil until reduced to a sauce-like consistency. Season with salt and pepper to taste and allow to cool. Meanwhile, heat the oven to 180°C/Gas 4.

Check the fish for any small bones, removing any with tweezers, then cut into 3cm chunks. Add to the sauce with the lemon juice and herbs, toss to mix, then pour into an earthenware baking dish. Bake for about 15 minutes.

Meanwhile, roll out the pastry and cut out 4 oval shapes, using an individual pie dish as a guide. Place on a baking sheet and brush with eggwash to glaze.

Remove the fish from the oven and keep warm. Raise the oven temperature to 200°C/Gas 6, then bake the pastry ovals for 7–10 minutes until golden brown.

Spoon the fish and creamy sauce on to warm plates, top with the oval pastry 'lids' and serve.

"As a lad growing up in Scotland, I loved fishing and learnt to respect the industry. I still get a thrill from catching my own fish and cooking it. Very fresh fish doesn't smell or feel slimy. It has bright eyes and firm flesh. Ask your fishmonger for his best catch of the day. If he fillets the fish for you, then ask for the trimmings to make your own fish stock"

"Look for traditionally cured bacon produced from a suitable pig, such as an English saddleback or Sussex Black. Mass-produced bacon contains chemicals and water, shrinks to nothing and is quite tasteless"

roast pheasant

WITH CREAMED CABBAGE AND BACON

Serves 4–6

1 brace of pheasants

olive oil to brush

4 thyme sprigs, leaves
   stripped

2 bay leaves

10 dry-cured smoked
   streaky bacon rashers

200ml double cream

½ head of Savoy cabbage,
   cored

½ head of white cabbage,
   cored

sea salt and pepper

Heat the oven to 190°C/Gas 5. Brush the pheasants with olive oil, sprinkle with the thyme leaves and lay a bay leaf on top of each pheasant. Wrap 3 bacon rashers over each pheasant to keep the breast moist (and hold the bay leaf in place) and place in a roasting pan. De-rind the other rashers, cut into lardons and set aside.

Roast the pheasant in the middle of the oven for 45 minutes, then remove the bacon and roast for a further 15 minutes until the skin is golden. Allow to rest in a warm place for 15 minutes.

Cook the bacon lardons in a dry pan for a couple of minutes, then add the cream and simmer gently for 5 minutes.

Meanwhile, finely shred both cabbages and blanch in boiling salted water for a few minutes until just tender. Drain thoroughly and add to the bacon and cream mixture. Season with salt and pepper.

Carve the pheasant at the table and serve with the creamed cabbage.

chicken casserole
WITH CORIANDER DUMPLINGS

Put the chicken in a large oval casserole, add the stock and bring to the boil. Add the vegetables and bring back to a simmer. Add the herbs, ginger and plenty of seasoning. Cover and simmer very gently for about 40 minutes until the chicken is tender. Remove from the heat and allow to cool. (This can be done a day in advance.)

Skim off any fat from the surface of the casserole. Lift out the chicken pieces, remove the meat from the bone, discard the skin, then return to the pan. Check the seasoning.

To make the coriander dumplings, mix the flour, suet and coriander together in a bowl, adding enough cold water to form a soft pliable dough. Shape into small dumplings.

Reheat the casserole. When the liquid comes to a boil, drop in the dumplings. Lower heat, re-cover and simmer for 10–15 minutes or until the dumplings are doubled in size and fluffy. Discard ginger and herbs.

Serve in warm pasta bowls, with crusty bread for mopping up the juices.

Serves 4–6

8–12 chicken portions (legs, thighs etc)
1 litre chicken stock
4 celery sticks, halved
2 leeks (white part only), finely chopped
2 red onions, cut into wedges
4 carrots, chopped
2 parsnips, chopped
1 celeriac, finely diced
1 bay leaf
few thyme sprigs
1 lemongrass stalk
knob of fresh root ginger, bruised
sea salt and pepper

Coriander dumplings:

250g plain flour
100g shredded suet
3 tbsp chopped coriander

"This is how every carrot should look – firm, with green leafy stalks attached. Whenever you buy carrots, always choose organic. Not only is the flavour far superior, it is the only way you can be sure that they are free from pesticides"

chicken casserole

braised shin of beef

WITH BABY TURNIPS AND MANGETOUT

Serves 4–6

2 tbsp olive oil

2kg shin of beef (on the bone)

3–4 garlic cloves, peeled

1 onion, roughly chopped

1 carrot, sliced

2 celery sticks, halved

1 turnip, chopped

1 beef tomato, deseeded and
   roughly chopped

600ml red wine

600ml beef stock

1 bay leaf

2 thyme sprigs

1 star anise

1 tsp coriander seeds

sea salt and pepper

200g baby turnips, trimmed

200g mangetout

Heat the olive oil in a large casserole, add the beef and sear on all sides; remove and set aside. Add the garlic, onion, carrot, celery, chopped turnip and tomato, and sweat for 3–5 minutes to soften.

Return the meat to the casserole, pour in the red wine and bring to the boil, then add the stock. Bring back to the boil, then add the bay leaf, thyme, star anise and coriander seeds. Reduce the heat to a low simmer, cover and cook gently for 2–3 hours until the meat is tender.

Carefully lift out the meat and allow to cool. Strain the cooking liquid through a chinois into a clean pan, discarding the vegetables. Skim off the fat, then boil until the stock is reduced to a sauce-like consistency. Season with salt and pepper to taste. Meanwhile, take the cooled meat off the bone, discarding all fat and sinew.

Cook the baby turnips in boiling salted water for 5–7 minutes until tender. Blanch the mangetout for 2 minutes. Drain.

Add the meat to the reduced liquor and warm through gently. Serve on warm plates with the turnips and mangetout, and plenty of mash.

"The flavour of Aberdeen Angus beef organically raised on good grazing pastures is amazing. How an animal lives, eats and is slaughtered is as important as the breed of the animal to the taste of the meat. Fergal, the handsome bull pictured above, lives on a farm in Devon "

saddle of lamb

STUFFED WITH SPINACH

Heat the oven to 200°C/Gas 6. Open out the saddle of lamb; set aside the eye fillets. Halve the garlic, season and leave for a few minutes to draw out the juices.

For the stuffing, heat a splash of olive oil in a non stick pan and sauté the mushrooms until softened and browned; drain in a colander. Heat a little more oil and a knob of butter in the pan, add the spinach, season lightly and cook until just wilted. Tip the mushrooms into a bowl, mix in the spinach, mascarpone and egg yolk, and season with nutmeg, salt and pepper.

Oil several sage leaves and place down the middle of the lamb. Rub the meat with the garlic bulb. Spoon the stuffing on top of the sage leaves. Cut the eye fillets horizontally (but not right through), open out and place over the stuffing. Fold one flap of the saddle over, then the other, wrapping firmly to make a neat roll. Secure with string at intervals and tuck the remaining sage leaves in at the ends.

Heat a splash of oil in a roasting pan, add the garlic bulb and sage sprigs and sauté briefly, then add the butter and allow to foam. Put the meat on top.

Roast for 30 minutes, then lower setting to 180°C/ Gas 4 and roast for a further 30 minutes. Lift meat on to a warm platter and rest in a warm place for 20 minutes. Deglaze pan juices with sherry vinegar, add the wine and stock, and reduce by half. Strain and adjust seasoning. Serve the lamb thickly sliced, with the jus.

Serves 6–8

1 saddle of lamb, about
  2.4kg, boned out
1 garlic bulb
sea salt and pepper
splash of olive oil
few sage sprigs
knob of butter

Stuffing:

3–4 tbsp olive oil
250g mixed mushrooms,
  (shiitake, oyster, button),
  cleaned
knob of butter
250g young spinach, stalks
  removed
2–3 tbsp mascarpone
1 egg yolk
freshly grated nutmeg
6–8 sage leaves

Pan jus:

1 tbsp sherry vinegar
2 glasses red wine
125ml light stock

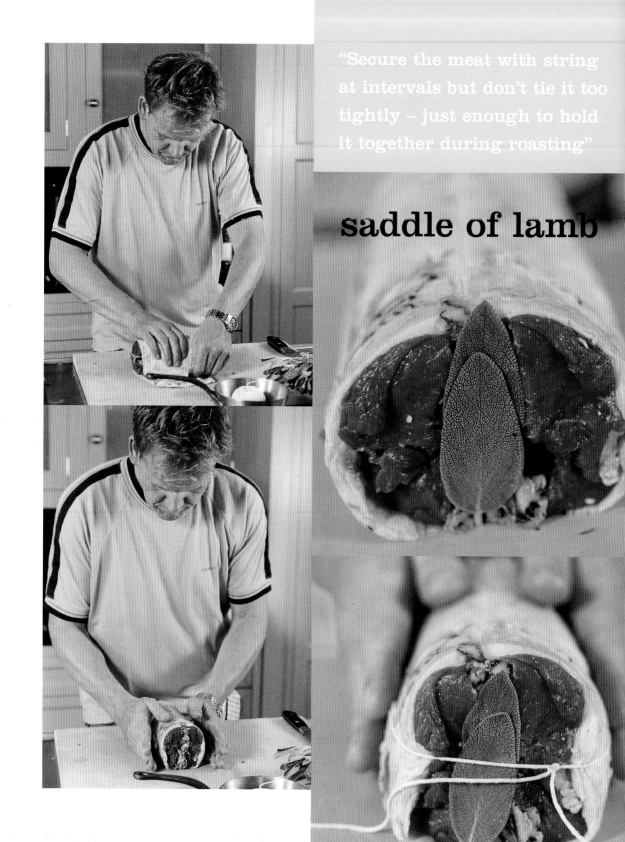

"Secure the meat with string at intervals but don't tie it too tightly – just enough to hold it together during roasting"

saddle of lamb

roast pork belly

WITH SAGE AND THYME

Serves 4–6

1kg boned piece of pork
  belly, skinned
sea salt and pepper
few thyme leaves
handful of sage leaves,
  roughly chopped
2–3 tbsp olive oil

Heat the oven to 220°C/Gas 7. Lay the pork, skinned-side up, on a board and season well with salt. Turn the meat, season with pepper and scatter the herbs over. Roll up from a long side and tie with string.

Heat the olive oil in a roasting pan on the hob, add the pork and sear on all sides. Transfer to the oven and roast for 10 minutes, then lower the setting to 150°C/Gas 2 and cook for a further 2 hours. Rest in a warm place for 10 minutes, then carve into slices. Serve with flavoured mash, baby carrots and cabbage.

creamy spinach tart

Roll out the pastry and line a 23cm flan tin, leaving some pastry overhanging the edge. Prick the base with a fork, line with greaseproof paper and fill with dried beans or rice. Chill for 20 minutes. Meanwhile, heat the oven to 200°C/Gas 6.

Steam the spinach (or cook in a pan with the minimum of water) until just wilted. Drain and set aside to cool.

Bake the pastry case for 15 minutes, then remove the paper and beans, and brush the base with the eggwash. Bake for a further 5 minutes. Allow to cool slightly, then trim the edge of the pastry level with the tin, using a very sharp knife. Lower the oven temperature to 180°C/Gas 4.

Lightly whisk the eggs and extra yolk together. Beat in the milk, crème fraîche, sea salt, cayenne and nutmeg. Mix in the spinach and pour into the pastry case. Bake for 25–35 minutes or until golden brown and set. Allow to cool slightly.

Serve the tart warm, cut into wedges, garnished with tomato slices.

Serves 4–6

300g ready-made shortcrust
  pastry
150g baby spinach, stalks
  removed
1 egg yolk, beaten with
  1 tsp water (eggwash)
2 large free-range eggs, plus
  1 extra egg yolk
100ml milk
300g crème fraîche
sea salt
1/2 tsp cayenne pepper
1/2 tsp freshly grated
  nutmeg
1 vine-ripened beef tomato,
  sliced, to garnish

rosemary potato galette

Serves 4

4 large potatoes, peeled

100g unsalted butter

4-6 rosemary sprigs, leaves
   stripped, plus extra sprigs
   to garnish

3-4 thyme sprigs, leaves
   stripped

sea salt and pepper

Slice the potatoes very thinly. Melt half the butter in a 25cm cast-iron frying pan. Take off the heat and arrange a third of the potato slices in an overlapping layer to cover the base of the pan. Sprinkle with half the rosemary and thyme leaves and season well. Dot with half the remaining butter.

Repeat these layers, then cover with the rest of the potato slices, season generously and press well down.

Cook on a low heat (or bake at 180°C/Gas 4) for 40–45 minutes until golden brown underneath. Invert the potato on to a plate and then slide back into the pan (this isn't necessary if you are baking the galette in the oven). Cook for a further 10–15 minutes.

Scatter a few rosemary sprigs over the galette and serve, cut into wedges.

stuffed baby squash

Slice the top off each squash, and cut another slice off the base, leaving 2cm thick shells. Scoop out and chop the flesh; set aside. Heat the oven to 200°C/Gas 6. Put the squash shells on a baking tray, brush with oil and season well. Bake for 5 minutes; let cool.

Peel and thickly slice the artichokes and immerse in a bowl of water, with the lemon juice added, to prevent discolouration.

Sauté the onion in 2 tbsp olive oil until soft. Stir in the celeriac and drained artichokes, then add the wine and 200ml stock. Simmer for 8–10 minutes until the vegetables are tender but still have a bite. Drain, reserving the stock, and tip into a bowl.

Sauté the chopped squash in 1 tbsp olive oil and half the butter for 2–3 minutes, then add the remaining 100ml stock and simmer for 6–8 minutes until very tender. Strain into a small pan, discarding the squash. Add the reserved stock and bubble to reduce by half. Stir in the cream and reduce again by half. Check the seasoning and add half the herbs.

Sauté the mushrooms in the remaining butter for a minute. Add to the bowl of vegetables with a little of the sauce to bind. Spoon into the squash shells and heat through in the oven for 5–6 minutes.

Warm the sauce and add the remaining herbs. Lift the baked squash shells on to warm plates. Using a spatula, spoon the sauce over and around, then serve.

Serves 4

4 baby acorn squash

3 tbsp olive oil, plus extra to brush

sea salt and pepper

250g Jerusalem artichokes

2 tbsp lemon juice

1 small onion, finely chopped

1 small celeriac, finely diced

100ml dry white wine

300ml vegetable stock or water

100g butter

100ml double cream

1 tbsp finely chopped parsley

1 tbsp finely chopped chervil

125g mixed wild mushrooms

stuffed
baby
squash

"I first started to appreciate squash in Australia and the USA, where it has been popular for decades. This versatile vegetable is increasingly popular here, and you can now find a good variety of squash, including acorn, butternut and turk's head"

gordon's trifle

Serves 6

1½ tbsp cornflour

300ml milk

2 vanilla pods, seeds
    removed

40g caster sugar

2 egg yolks

225g strawberries

150g raspberries

130g Madeira sponge

300ml double cream

Mix the cornflour with a little of the milk in a pan until smooth, then add the rest of the milk with the vanilla pods and half the sugar. Slowly bring to the boil, stirring continuously, then take off the heat.

Whisk the egg yolks in a bowl, using an electric whisk, until pale in colour, then gradually whisk in the hot milk mixture.

Return to the pan and stir over a very low heat for 2 minutes; don't let it boil or the custard will curdle. Take off the heat, cover the surface with damp greaseproof paper and allow to cool.

Purée 100g strawberries and 40g raspberries in a blender or food processor with the remaining sugar and 75ml water. Transfer to a bowl and stir in most of the remaining berries, reserving some for decoration. Spoon into a glass serving bowl. Cut the sponge into 2cm squares and scatter over the fruit.

Whip the cream until softly peaking. Remove the vanilla pods from the cooled custard, then fold in the whipped cream. Spoon over the sponge and spread evenly. Chill for 1 hour or until ready to serve.

Scatter the reserved berries over the top of the trifle to serve.

steamed apricot pudding

Serves 4–6

10 fresh apricots

butter to grease

100g self-raising flour

125g shredded suet

3 free-range eggs

finely grated zest of
   $\frac{1}{2}$ lemon

$\frac{1}{2}$ tsp baking powder

60g fresh white
   breadcrumbs

Sauce:

30g unsalted butter,
   softened

65g light muscovado sugar

75ml apricot purée (see
   recipe)

50ml double cream

Halve and stone the apricots, then cut off a third of each half horizontally from the base to give a rounded slice. Butter a 1.2 litre pudding basin. Arrange the rounded apricot slices in the bottom of the basin and a little way up the sides.

Purée the rest of the apricots in a blender or food processor. Measure 100ml apricot purée for the pudding. Keep the rest (about 75ml) for the sauce.

Put the flour, suet, eggs and lemon zest in the food processor and process for 30 seconds. Add the baking powder, apricot purée and breadcrumbs, and whiz for a further 30 seconds. Carefully spoon the mixture into the basin.

Cover the top of the basin generously with a double layer of greaseproof paper, making a pleat in the centre. Secure under the rim with string. Place in a saucepan containing enough boiling water to come halfway up the side, cover tightly and steam for 2 hours, topping up the boiling water as necessary. (Or cook in an electric steamer for $1\frac{1}{2}$ hours.)

To make the sauce, gently melt the butter in a small pan, add the sugar and stir until dissolved. Increase the heat slightly and cook to a treacle-like consistency. Take off the heat and stir in the apricot purée and cream; keep warm.

Turn the pudding out on to a warm plate, pour over the apricot sauce and serve immediately.

pan-roasted apples and pears
WITH BRAMBLE SYRUP

Serves 4

2 large Cox's apples

2 large Conference or
 Williams pears

4 tbsp icing sugar, sifted

200g blackberries

250ml stock syrup (see
 page 248)

2 tbsp Poire eau-de-vie or
 Calvados (optional)

mint sprigs to serve

Core and slice the apples and pears, but don't peel them. Heat a large, heavy-based frying pan until you see a faint haze rising.

Toss the sliced fruits in icing sugar, then immediately put into the pan in a single layer. Leave for a few seconds until the undersides begin to caramelise, then turn and lightly caramelise the other side for a few seconds. Don't overcook – the fruit should still be firm.

Tip the blackberries into a large bowl and lightly crush with a potato masher. Add the caramelised apples and pears, pour the stock syrup and alcohol over, and toss gently. Leave to cool, then cover and chill for 2 hours.

Spoon the fruit and liquor into glass dishes and top with mint sprigs to serve.

"I use this technique for peaches, nectarines and mangoes as well. Caramelised fruit is also the basis of my tart tatins: Use an ovenproof pan for pan-frying, then cover the fruits with a sheet of puff pastry and bake at 200°C/Gas 6 for 10–15 minutes. Invert on to a plate to serve"

"There's something very satisfying about picking fruit from the hedgerows and transforming it into delectable desserts, jellies and jams, that is of course if you live in the country. Otherwise, farmer's markets and pick-your-own-fruit farms are a good source of seasonal soft fruits"

summer
barbies

When I'm relaxing at home in the summer, I invariably fire up the barbecue. It's such a great way to bring out the flavour of food and shouldn't be limited to burgers and sausages. Fish, meat, vegetables and fruit all lend themselves to barbecuing. Marinating food in advance adds flavour and keeps leaner cuts succulent. Use good sturdy tongs, long-handled forks and gloves to ensure that you don't burn yourself. Barbecues are an excellent way to entertain – especially if you get everyone involved in the cooking.

"I like to serve these juicy tiger prawns with a spiked vinaigrette for dipping. Just flavour 150ml classic vinaigrette with 1 chopped, deseeded red chilli, 1 finely chopped lemongrass stalk and a squeeze of lemon juice"

"This spice paste also works well with chunky fish fillets and chicken pieces. Remember that barbecue coals need to be white, with no flame, or you will scorch the food before it's properly cooked"

seared tiger prawns
WITH GARLIC, CHILLI AND LEMONGRASS

Serves 4-6

12 large, raw tiger prawns,
   peeled and deveined (tail
   shell on)
2-3 garlic cloves, peeled
2 red chillies, deseeded
2 lemongrass stalks
2.5cm piece fresh root
   ginger, peeled
4-6 tbsp olive oil
sea salt and pepper

Put the tiger prawns in a shallow dish. Pound the garlic, chillies, lemongrass and ginger together using a pestle and mortar, gradually adding the olive oil until you have a rough paste (or whiz briefly in a blender). Season with salt and pepper. Baste the prawns with the spice paste and leave to marinate in a cool place for 2-3 hours.

Cook the marinated prawns on the hot barbecue for 4-6 minutes, turning, until they turn pink and feel slightly firm to the touch – don't overcook. Serve at once, with a flavoured vinaigrette, soured cream or tomato salsa.

barbecued whole sea bream
IN BANANA LEAVES WITH CHILLI

Serves 4 8

4 sea bream, about
    500–600g each, scaled,
    gutted and cleaned
4 large banana leaves
olive oil to brush
a little sesame oil
4 red chillies, deseeded and
    chopped
2 lemongrass stalks
2–3 garlic cloves, roughly
    chopped
2.5cm piece fresh root
    ginger, sliced
sea salt and pepper
handful of coriander leaves,
    chopped
juice of 2 limes
600ml coconut milk

Slash the skin of the fish 3 or 4 times on both sides. Lay the banana leaves on a surface, brush lightly with olive oil, then sprinkle with a little sesame oil. Lay a sea bream across the centre of each leaf. (If you can't find banana leaves, use foil instead.)

Mix the chillies, lemongrass, garlic and ginger together, and press into the slashes in the fish. Season with salt and pepper, scatter the coriander over the fish and drizzle with the lime juice.

Wrap each fish in a banana leaf, folding in the ends like an envelope. Carefully pour the coconut milk into the parcel (find a gap to do so), then secure with string. (Should any of the banana leaves split, simply overwrap in foil.)

Place the fish parcels on the barbecue and cook for 25–30 minutes or until the flesh is opaque. Test by inserting a knife – the flesh should lift cleanly from the bone.

To serve, open out the banana leaf and carefully lift the fish fillets from the bone. Hot new potatoes and a simple green salad are ideal accompaniments.

lemon chilli chicken wings

WITH A COUSCOUS SALAD

Serves 4–6

8–12 chicken wings

juice of 1 lemon, skins
    reserved

9 tbsp olive oil

2 red chillies, chopped

2 green chillies, chopped

2 red peppers

2 green peppers

3 garlic cloves (unpeeled)

200g couscous

1 tsp ground cumin

sea salt and pepper

120g cherry tomatoes,
    halved

large handful of coriander
    leaves, chopped

Toss the chicken wings with half the lemon juice, 4 tbsp of the olive oil, the chopped chillies and spent lemon skins in a bowl. Cover and leave to marinate in the fridge for 2–3 hours.

Meanwhile, heat the oven to 200°C/Gas 6. Toss the whole peppers and garlic cloves with 4 tbsp olive oil and roast on a baking tray for 15–20 minutes or until the skins are scorched and wrinkled. Leave to cool on the tray.

Put the couscous in a bowl and pour on 200ml boiling water. Stir with a fork, then leave to stand for 20 minutes, forking through the couscous every 5 minutes or so, to ensure that the grains separate and the couscous is fluffy. Sprinkle in the cumin and add the remaining olive oil and lemon juice. Fork through, seasoning liberally with salt and pepper.

Peel the roasted peppers, then tear open, remove the seeds and chop the flesh. Squeeze the soft pulp from the garlic skins and mix into the couscous with the chopped peppers and halved cherry tomatoes. Mix in the chopped coriander to taste.

Cook the chicken wings on the barbecue, turning and basting regularly with the marinade until brown, crisp and cooked through. Serve in bowls on a bed of couscous salad.

wild boar sausages
WITH CHIANTI SAUCE

Serves 4–6

500g wild boar sausages

Sauce:

150g unsalted butter, chilled and diced

3 shallots, thinly sliced

1 garlic clove, crushed

few thyme sprigs

500ml Chianti or similar red wine

1 tbsp brown sugar

1 tsp Dijon mustard

splash of balsamic vinegar

sea salt and pepper

Have the sausages ready at room temperature, but don't prick them (as you want to keep the fat within to baste them naturally on the barbecue).

To make the sauce, melt a knob of the butter in a pan, then add the shallots, garlic and thyme. Cook over a high heat for a few minutes, then add the wine and sugar and bring to the boil, stirring to dissolve the sugar. Boil steadily until reduced by half. Discard the thyme.

Take the sauce off the heat and whisk in the mustard and cold butter, a piece at a time. Add the balsamic vinegar and season with salt and pepper to taste.

Barbecue the sausages slowly on a medium heat until nicely coloured and cooked through. Serve on a bed of herb-flavoured mashed potato, with the Chianti sauce and crusty bread on the side.

barbecued steaks

WITH A PIQUANT RED PEPPER SAUCE

Serves 4–6

4–6 sirloin or rib eye steaks,
   about 200g each

2 tsp paprika

2 tsp pink peppercorns,
   lightly crushed

1 glass red wine

6–7 tbsp olive oil

2 red peppers

4 garlic cloves (unpeeled)

2 lemons

sea salt and pepper

Lay the steaks in a shallow dish and sprinkle with 1 tsp paprika and the pink peppercorns. Pour on the wine and 2 tbsp olive oil, then cover and leave to marinate at room temperature for 1 hour.

Meanwhile, heat the oven to 200°C/Gas 6. Toss the whole peppers and garlic cloves with 2 tbsp olive oil and roast on a baking tray for 15–20 minutes or until the skin is scorched and wrinkled. Leave to cool on the tray.

Squeeze the garlic pulp out of the skins into a blender or food processor. Peel the roasted peppers, open and remove the seeds, then add to the blender with any juices. Whiz to a smooth paste.

With the motor running, add 1 tsp paprika, the juice of $\frac{1}{2}$ lemon and 2–3 tbsp olive oil, processing to emulsify. Season with salt and pepper to taste.

Cut the other 1½ lemons into fairly thick slices, removing the pips.

Cook the steaks on the barbecue over a high heat, along with the lemon slices. Allow 3–5 minutes on each side, then allow to rest on a warm plate for about 5 minutes. Serve topped with the lemon slices and accompanied by the sauce.

"Look for well-hung steaks with a good dark colour and a marbling of fat. Aberdeen Angus beef is my favourite"

barnsley chops

"These double
loin chops
from the
saddle of lamb
are ideal for a
barbecue,
because the fat
is all around
the outside of
the chops and
prevents them
drying out"

Serves 4–6
4–6 Barnsley chops
1 tsp thin honey
1 glass red wine
pepper
Mint sauce:
2 tsp sugar
125ml white wine vinegar
1 shallot, finely chopped
large handful of mint leaves, finely chopped

Put the lamb chops in a shallow dish, drizzle with the honey, pour on the wine and grind over plenty of black pepper.

To make the sauce, combine the sugar, wine vinegar and shallot in a pan, bring to the boil and let bubble until reduced by half. Take off the heat, add the chopped mint and allow to cool.

Cook the chops on the barbecue for 4–6 minutes each side, basting with the marinade. Serve with the mint sauce.

barbecued fennel
WITH PERNOD AND STAR ANISE

"This dish is too good to be limited to the barbecue. To cook indoors, char-grill the fennel on an oiled griddle, then bake in a covered dish at 180°C/Gas 4 for around 30 minutes until tender and fragrant"

Serves 4–6

3 large fennel bulbs

2 celery sticks, finely sliced

2 star anise

sea salt and pepper

1 glass medium dry white wine

shot of Pernod

5 knobs of butter

2–3 garlic cloves, chopped

small handful of tarragon and parsley, chopped

Cut the fennel from top to root into thin slices and cut out the tough core. Have ready a large square of foil.

Char-grill the fennel slices briefly on the barbecue, turning once, then transfer to the middle of the foil. Scatter the celery over, add the star anise and season with salt and pepper. Pour over the wine and drizzle with a little Pernod. Dot with the butter and chopped garlic, then scatter the herbs over.

Wrap the fennel in the foil to make a parcel, then place on the edge of the barbecue. Leave to cook slowly for 20–25 minutes, then open up the parcel and serve.

grilled flat mushrooms
WITH MASCARPONE, BLUE CHEESE AND BASIL

Serves 4

4 large, flat field
  mushrooms
1 tbsp olive oil
125g mascarpone
75g Stilton or other blue
  cheese, crumbled
pepper
handful of basil leaves,
  chopped

Wipe the mushrooms with a damp piece of kitchen paper or use a soft brush to remove any dirt or grit, but don't wash them. Cut out the stalks.

Brush a large sheet of foil with the olive oil and place the mushrooms, gill-side up, in the middle.

Mix the mascarpone with the blue cheese and season with plenty of pepper. Fill the mushroom caps with this mixture and sprinkle with chopped basil.

Keeping the stuffed mushrooms flat, bring up two opposite sides of the foil and fold the edges together, then seal the ends of the parcel. Place on the edge of the barbecue to cook for 10–15 minutes (or you could cook in the oven at 180°C/Gas 4).

Serve as a starter with sourdough bread, or as an accompaniment to barbecued meats.

"I adore mushrooms, especially those gathered as they grow naturally in woods and fields. I often chat to the mushroom pickers who bring samples into the restaurant – it's as though they belong to a secret club. We buy their mushrooms and use them on the menu, but I know what we pay is a pittance for the time they take collecting them"

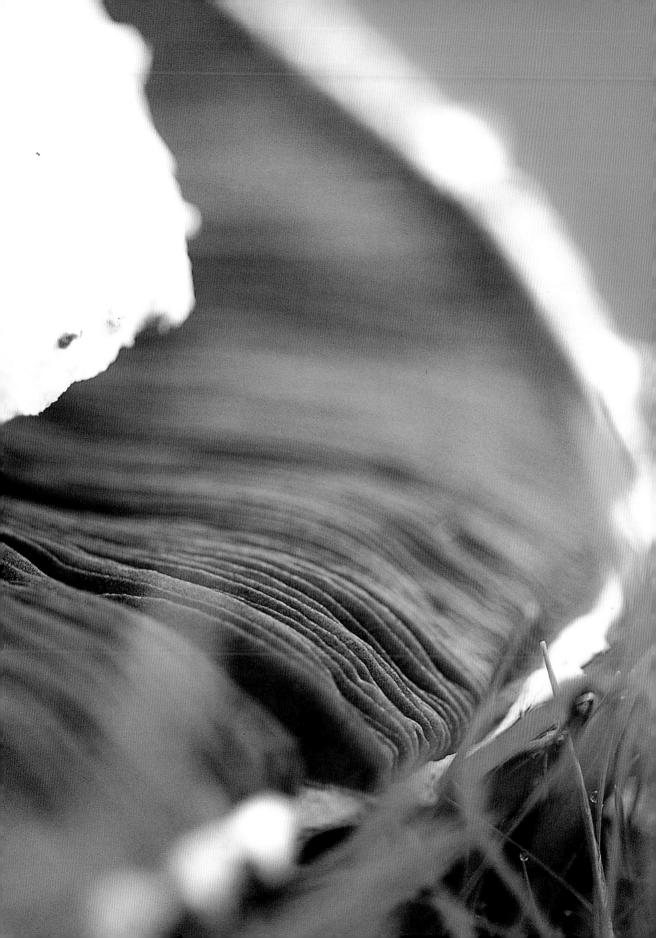

lemon tart

WITH A CARAMELISED TOPPING

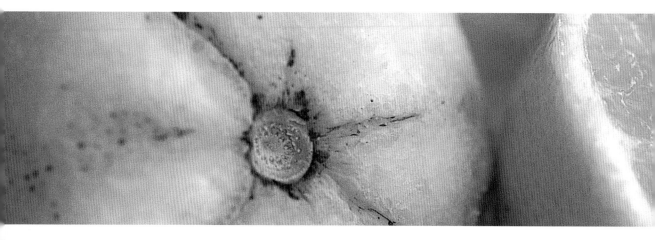

Roll out the pastry thinly and use to line a 20cm tart tin placed on a baking sheet. Press well into the edges and leave the excess pastry overhanging the edge. Line with greaseproof paper and fill with dried beans or rice. Chill for 20 minutes. Heat the oven to 180°C/Gas 4.

Bake the tart for 12–15 minutes. Remove the paper and beans and bake for a further 5 minutes. Allow to cool, then trim the pastry level with the top of the tin. Turn the oven down to 100°C/Gas ¼.

To make the filling, put the lemon juice, caster sugar, egg yolks, double cream and 110ml water in a bowl and whisk with a fork to combine, but do not overwork.

Place the tart tin on the middle oven shelf and carefully pour in the filling. Bake for 45–50 minutes, then turn out the oven and leave the tart inside to cool very slowly. (The filling will be slightly wobbly when you turn the oven off.) When completely cold, chill the tart for 1–2 hours until set.

Dust the surface with icing sugar and caramelise with a cook's blowtorch. Leave until the topping is cool and crisp, then dust again and caramelise. Serve at once.

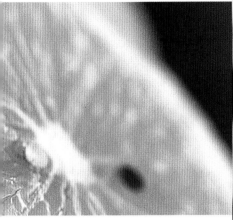

Serves 4–6

1 quantity of sweet flan
  pastry (see overleaf)

Filling:

juice of $1\frac{1}{2}$ lemons

180g caster sugar

6 free-range egg yolks,
  beaten

150ml double cream

icing sugar to dust

Sweet Flan Pastry
is easy to make in a
food processor – just
take care to avoid
overworking it.
Put 125g unsalted
butter (at room
temperature) and 90g
caster sugar in the
processor and whiz
until just combined,
then add 1 free-range
large egg and whiz for
30 seconds. Add 250g
plain flour and process
briefly until the dough
just comes together.
Knead lightly on a
floured surface, then
wrap in cling film and
rest in the fridge for
30 minutes before
rolling out.

"Like strawberries, redcurrants are synonymous with an English summer. Counter their slight tartness by frosting in caster sugar, and use to decorate desserts and cakes"

summer strawberry salad
WITH CHAMPAGNE GRANITA

Serves 4–6
400g strawberries, sliced
few lemon balm leaves,
   shredded
125g redcurrants
caster sugar to coat
Champagne granita:
125g sugar
juice of 1 lemon
3 tbsp liquid glucose
250ml Champagne

To make the granita, put the sugar, lemon juice and liquid glucose in a pan with 250ml water and heat gently until the sugar has dissolved. Bring to the boil and simmer for 3 minutes. Allow to cool.

Stir the Champagne into the cooled sugar syrup, then pour into a freezerproof container. Freeze for 2–3 hours, forking the mixture every hour to break up the ice crystals.

Arrange the strawberry slices on a large platter and sprinkle with the lemon balm. Scrape shavings off the granita and scatter over the top. Dip the redcurrants into the caster sugar and arrange on the salad. Serve immediately.

just for
kids

Getting children involved in the kitchen from an early age encourages them to appreciate good food. It's amazing how much more a child enjoys eating food they've helped to prepare, or perhaps grow in the garden. Watching them make their own burgers and pizzas is so rewarding – matched by the pure delight on their faces as they later devour them. I get them to think about what they are eating and where it comes from. This year they are all growing tomatoes in the garden ... it could become competitive.

chunky vegetable soup

> "Brimming with vegetables, this is the ideal food for hungry kids returning home from school. Even a child who hates veggies may be tempted. Plenty of crusty bread turns the soup into a meal in its own right"

Serves 4–6

1.2 litres vegetable stock
4 celery sticks, finely sliced
1 onion, diced
2 carrots, diced
1 turnip, diced
1 sweet potato, diced
400g can butter beans, drained
sea salt and pepper
2 tbsp chopped flat-leaf parsley
olive oil to drizzle
freshly grated Parmesan to serve

Heat the stock in a large saucepan. Add the celery, onion, carrots, turnip and sweet potato, and bring to the boil. Lower the heat, cover and simmer for 20 minutes.

Add the butter beans and simmer for a further 10 minutes. Season with salt and pepper to taste. Whiz briefly, using a stick blender, to purée a little of the soup and thicken the liquor slightly, but keep a good chunky consistency.

Stir in the parsley and check the seasoning. Spoon the soup into warm bowls, drizzle with a little olive oil and serve sprinkled with Parmesan.

tomato and mozzarella pizza
WITH VARIOUS TOPPINGS

Serves 4–8

Dough:

2 tsp fast-action dried yeast

250ml tepid water

600g strong plain (bread)
  flour

1 tbsp olive oil

Tomato base:

560g jar passata

knob of butter

1 garlic clove, crushed

sea salt and pepper

Toppings:

100g bocconcini (mozzarella
  balls), halved

300g cherry tomatoes,
  halved

small handful of basil
  leaves, roughly torn

100g pepperoni sausage
  (optional)

small jar or tub of olives
  (optional)

sea salt and pepper

freshly shaved Parmesan

To make the dough, add the yeast to the warm water, stir and leave to stand for a few minutes. Tip the flour into a food processor, add the oil, then with the motor running, pour in the yeast liquid. Process until the dough is smooth and leaves the side of the bowl clean. Transfer to a bowl, cover with cling film and leave in a warm place until doubled in volume.

To make the tomato base, place the passata, butter and garlic in a small pan over a medium-high heat. Bring to a simmer and cook until reduced by half. Season with salt and pepper to taste.

Put all the topping ingredients in bowls on the kitchen table. Heat the oven to 220°C/Gas 7. Cut the pizza dough in half.

Roll out the pizza dough, one portion at a time, on a lightly floured surface to a large round – making it as thin as possible. Place each round on a heavy baking sheet (or a large cast-iron frying pan suitable for use in your oven if you have one). Spread with the tomato base.

Top with the mozzarella, cherry tomatoes and basil. Add other toppings as you like, season and scatter over some grated Parmesan. Better, still, get the children to apply their own choice of ingredients.

Bake for 8–10 minutes, until golden, then cut each pizza into 4 wedges and serve.

"Pizzas are deceptively easy to make at home and healthier than a take-away. There's no limit to the toppings you can apply – seafood and pan-roasted vegetables are tasty options"

"I'm a great believer in getting children involved in preparing food, and homemade pizzas are a brilliant way of encouraging them to try different ingredients"

salmon fish cakes

Serves 4–8

600g floury potatoes, such as Desirée,
   peeled and cut into even-sized pieces

sea salt and pepper

large knob of butter

1 onion, finely chopped

2 tbsp olive oil

400g salmon fillet, skinned

1 free-range egg yolk

1 free-range egg, beaten

100g natural breadcrumbs

groundnut oil to fry

"To make these appealing to young children, make fish-shaped cakes. When cooked, add a little red pepper eye to each one ... guaranteed to raise a smile"

Boil the potatoes in salted water until soft, then drain and press through a potato ricer into a large bowl (or mash well). Beat in the butter and seasoning.

Fry the onion in the olive oil until soft but not coloured, then add to the potato mixture. Check the salmon fillet for small bones, removing any with tweezers.

Purée a quarter of the salmon in a food processor, then beat into the potato mixture with the egg yolk. Finely dice the remaining salmon and fold into the potato mixture. Cover and chill for 30 minutes.

Shape the mixture into 8 fish cakes. Dip first into the beaten egg and then into the breadcrumbs to coat. Place on a tray and chill for a further 30–40 minutes.

Heat a thin film of groundnut oil in a large frying pan, add the fish cakes and fry for 2–3 minutes each side or until golden brown. Drain on kitchen paper. Serve with halved cherry tomatoes and cucumber.

pasta with bacon
AND PEAS

Serves 4-6

200g dried fusilli or other pasta shapes

sea salt and pepper

3 tbsp olive oil

1 onion, finely chopped

1 garlic clove, finely chopped

100g bacon lardons

300ml double cream

100g frozen peas

1–2 tbsp chopped flat-leaf parsley

1–2 tbsp freshly grated Parmesan

Cook the pasta in a large pan of boiling salted water with 1 tbsp olive oil for 7–10 minutes until al dente (cooked but firm to the bite). Drain and rinse under cold water to remove excess starch. Return to the pan and set aside.

Heat the remaining olive oil in a deep sauté pan. Add the onion and garlic and fry, stirring, for 2–3 minutes, then add the bacon and fry until crisp. Add the cream and let bubble until reduced by half.

Add the peas, bring back to a simmer and cook for 2 minutes. Season with salt and pepper to taste.

Add the pasta to the sauce and heat through, stirring, for 1–2 minutes. Scatter with parsley and Parmesan, and serve in warm pasta bowls.

"Pasta is a great energy booster and children love it. You'll probably find you have all the ingredients for this simple recipe in the kitchen ... and what's more it is nutritionally well balanced"

cheese toasties

Serves 4

225g Lancashire cheese,
  cut into cubes
1 free-range egg yolk
2–3 tsp Worcestershire
  sauce
½ tsp Dijon mustard
1–2 tbsp single cream
8 slices good-quality white
  bread
olive oil to fry

Put the cheese, egg yolk, Worcestershire sauce and mustard in a food processor. Whiz until smooth, adding enough cream to give a thick paste.

Spread the mixture on to 4 slices of bread and sandwich together with the other slices of bread. Remove the crusts and cut the sandwiches in half on the diagonal.

Heat a thin film of olive oil in a frying pan and cook the sandwiches for a minute or two on each side until golden brown. Drain on kitchen paper and serve wrapped in paper napkins.

mini meg burgers

> "All kids love burgers. They are so simple and quick to make that I fail to understand why parents ever buy processed patties packed with additives and preservatives"

Makes 6 mini-burgers

300g lean ground beef or minced rump steak

1 onion, finely chopped

pepper

2 tbsp olive oil

6 mini buns, split

1 tbsp mayonnaise

1 tbsp tomato ketchup

4 Cos lettuce leaves, shredded

10 cherry tomatoes, sliced

oven-roasted chips

To make your own chips, cut 2 clean, large baking potatoes into wedges, about 2cm thick. Add to a pan of boiling water and blanch for 4 minutes, then drain well. Return to the dry pan, add 2 tbsp olive oil and shake the pan to coat the chips in the oil. Spread the chips out on a baking tray and bake at 200°C/Gas 6 for 10 minutes. Shake the tray to turn the chips and bake for a further 10–15 minutes. or until crisp and golden brown. Drain the potato wedges on kitchen paper, season with salt and serve.

Put the ground beef and onion into a bowl and mix well, seasoning with pepper. Form into 6 balls, flatten slightly and wrap in cling film. Refrigerate for 30 minutes or until ready to cook. (This can be done a day ahead.)

Place a heavy-based frying pan (preferably cast-iron) over a high heat for 2–3 minutes and add the olive oil. When hot, add the burgers and press down gently. Cook for 3 minutes each side and then turn down the heat and cook for a further 5 minutes. Turn off the heat and leave the burgers to rest in the pan for 5 minutes.

Heat the grill and lightly toast the split buns on both sides. Mix the mayonnaise and ketchup together in a small bowl.

Put the shredded lettuce on the bun bases, top with the burgers, then cover with the sliced tomatoes. Spoon the ketchup mix on top, then sandwich together with the bun tops and press gently. Serve with homemade oven-roasted chips.

fruity yogurt lollies

Makes 4

1 large mango, 6 apricots or
  3 peaches, peeled, halved
  and stoned
65g caster sugar
500g natural yogurt

Whiz the fruit in a blender or food processor with 1 tbsp sugar until smooth. Pass through a sieve or mouli into a bowl, cover and refrigerate.

Tip the yogurt into a bowl, add the rest of the sugar and stir well to dissolve. Divide between 4 lolly moulds or strong plastic cups and place in the freezer for 1 hour.

Swirl the fruit purée into the semi-frozen yogurt (don't mix too thoroughly). Place a lolly stick or strong plastic spoon in the centre of each lolly and return to the freezer for 2 hours or until solid.

Store the lollies in a freezer bag (unless they are going to be eaten the same day). They will keep well for up to 2 months. To serve, allow to stand at room temperature for 5 minutes, then remove the moulds or cups. Watch the kids devour them!

fruit kebabs

WITH CHOCOLATE DIP

Serves 6–8

½ pineapple, peeled,
  halved and cored
2–3 bananas, peeled
3 kiwi fruit, peeled
12–16 strawberries
12–16 raspberries
12–16 blackberries
12–16 cherries, pitted
200g good-quality dark
  chocolate

Cut the pineapple, bananas and kiwi fruit into chunks and arrange them on a large platter with the various berries and cherries. Encourage the kids to thread their favourite fruits on to short wooden kebab skewers.

Melt the chocolate in a bowl set over a pan of gently simmering water. Stir until smooth, then pour into a couple of warm ramekins.

Serve the fruit kebabs with the warm chocolate for dipping.

banana split

Serves 4–6

750g strawberries

75g good-quality dark
   chocolate

4–6 medium bananas

300ml double cream

400g vanilla ice cream

Whiz half of the strawberries in a blender or food processor to a purée, then pass through a fine sieve into a bowl.

Break up the chocolate and put into a bowl set over a pan of gently simmering water. Leave until melted, then stir until smooth.

Halve the bananas lengthways and place, cut-side down, in shallow serving bowls. Set aside a handful of whole strawberries for serving. Slice the rest and scatter over the banana, then drizzle with half the melted chocolate.

Whip the cream until softly peaking. Place scoops of ice cream on top of the bananas, then spoon on the whipped cream. Drizzle with the strawberry purée and remaining melted chocolate. Top with the whole strawberries and serve.

"When I was a child we didn't eat out as a family very often, but when we did it was a huge treat. The best part for me was always the pudding and a banana split was my absolute favourite"

fruit and honey cereal bars

Makes 9 or 12

300g porridge oats

70g demerara sugar

3 tbsp thin honey

100g mixed dried tropical
  fruit, such as mango,
  pineapple and papaya,
  roughly chopped

100g unsalted butter

Heat the oven to 180°C/Gas 4. Line a shallow 20cm baking tin with baking parchment. Put the oats, sugar and honey into a large bowl, add the dried fruit and stir well.

Melt the butter in a pan over a low heat, then pour into the oat mixture and mix thoroughly. Tip into the lined tin and spread evenly. Press down firmly with the back of a spoon.

Bake in the oven for 20–25 minutes until golden brown. Leave to cool completely in the tin, then lift the baking paper to remove. Cut into squares or slices.

party biscuits

Makes 20–24

125g unsalted butter

125g caster sugar

1 egg, beaten

250g plain flour

½ tsp ground mixed spice

To decorate:

150g icing sugar

coloured sugar

silver balls (optional)

Cream the butter and sugar together in a bowl until creamy and soft. Gradually beat in the egg.

Sift the flour and spice together, then work into the mixture, using a metal spoon to begin with, then your hands. Gather the mixture together and knead for 1–2 minutes to make a smooth dough.

Wrap the dough in cling film and rest in the fridge for 30 minutes. Heat the oven to 180°C/Gas 4. Line a baking sheet with greaseproof paper. Divide the dough into 4 portions and re-wrap all but one.

Roll out the dough on a lightly floured surface to a 5–7mm thickness. Use biscuit cutters to cut out figures, stars or other shapes. At Christmas, use festive cutters (Christmas trees, etc.) and make a hole near the top with a skewer, so you can hang the biscuits on the tree. Place on the lined baking sheet. Repeat with the rest of the dough.

Bake for 10–15 minutes until the biscuits are pale golden in colour. Leave on the baking sheet for a few minutes to firm up, then lift on to a wire rack to cool.

To decorate the biscuits, mix the icing sugar with enough water to make a smooth, very thin glaze. Brush the biscuits with the icing glaze, using a pastry brush, and then sprinkle on the coloured sugar. Decorate with silver balls if you like. Leave on a wire rack until the icing is dry.

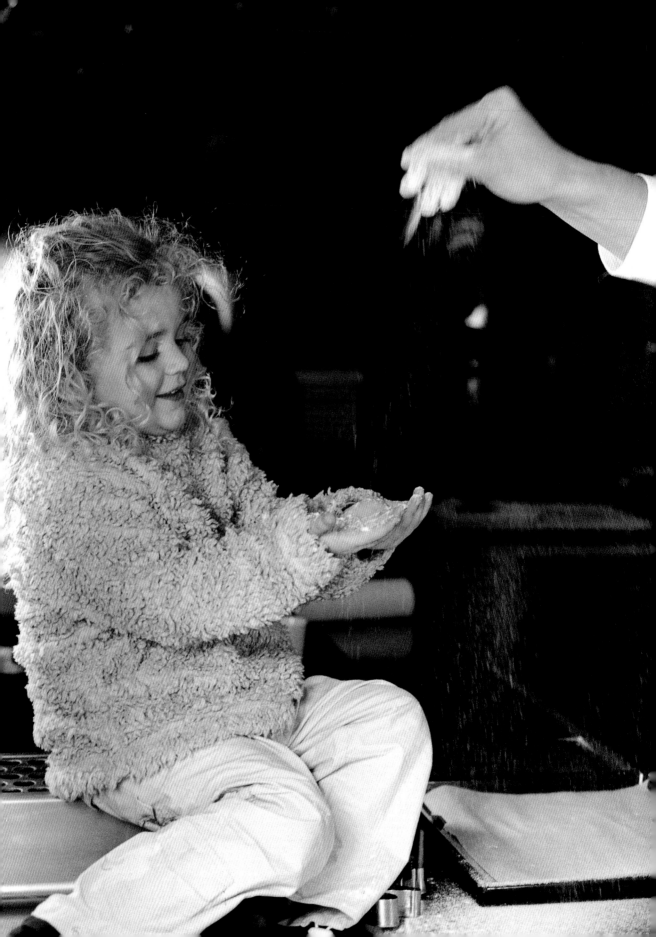

"Cooking with children is pure magic, I love to see the joy on their faces as they see the product of their work"

bellinis and blinis

When Tana and I throw a party, we never quite know how many we are catering for. Finger food with Champagne cocktails is an easy option. We make canapés in advance and treat ourselves as guests at our own party. We encourage friends to pass round trays of food and this gets them mingling. It never ceases to amaze me how much food is consumed. As a rough guide, I suggest you allow 7–10 canapés per person, depending on the time of day. Scatter bowls of olives and nuts around the room and keep everything relaxed.

hot-smoked salmon blinis

WITH CAPER BERRIES

Makes 25–40, depending on size

50g wholemeal flour

1 tbsp fast-action dried yeast

700ml tepid milk

125g buckwheat flour

125g plain flour

4 free-range eggs, separated

butter to fry

To serve:

200g kiln-roasted or hot-smoked salmon

125ml soured cream

caper berries

Put the wholemeal flour and yeast into a large mixing bowl and stir in 475ml milk. Stir well and leave in a warm place for 20 minutes.

In the meantime, flake the salmon along its natural contours, cover and set aside.

Add the buckwheat and plain flours, egg yolks and remaining 225ml milk to the yeast mixture and mix well until smooth. In another bowl, whisk the egg whites until softly peaking, then lightly fold into the yeast batter.

Cook the blinis in batches. Heat 1 tbsp butter in a blini pan or small non-stick frying pan. Drop small spoonfuls of batter into the pan, spacing them slightly apart. Cook for about $1^{1}/_{2}$ minutes until the surface is covered with tiny bubbles and the undersides are golden brown.

Flip the blinis over and cook for another minute, then transfer to a warm plate lined with kitchen paper; keep warm while you cook the rest.

Spoon a little soured cream on to each blini and top with a piece of salmon and a caper berry to serve.

mini tart tatins

OF CARAMELISED RED ONION AND GOAT'S CHEESE

"Blinis are great canapés and you can vary the toppings as you like. Use crème fraîche instead of soured cream if you prefer. For a glamorous finish, spoon on a little caviar or lumpfish roe instead of the caper berries"

Makes 24

2 tbsp olive oil

2 red onions, finely chopped

1 garlic clove, finely chopped

1 firm, ripe goat's cheese, about 125g, in pieces

200g ready-made puff pastry

Heat the oven to 200°C/Gas 6. Have ready two 12-hole non-stick mini muffin tins.

Heat the olive oil in a small frying pan and add the onions and garlic. Cook slowly for 5–8 minutes until the onions begin to caramelise. Spoon into the mini muffin tins and dot each with a little goat's cheese.

Roll out the puff pastry, then scrunch it up and roll it out again (this will prevent it from rising too much, which you want to avoid here). Cut out discs that will fit snugly over the filling in the muffin tins.

Place the pastry discs on top of the onion and press down firmly. Bake for 5–7 minutes until golden brown. Allow to stand for 5 minutes, then carefully turn out the tarts on to a wire rack. Serve warm.

roasted pumpkin crostini
WITH PANCETTA

Makes 20

1 small French stick

¼ peeled, deseeded
pumpkin (about 150g
prepared weight), finely
chopped

2 tbsp olive oil

sea salt and pepper

100g diced pancetta

freshly shaved Parmesan

Heat the oven to 180°C/Gas 4. Cut the bread into 1cm thick slices, place on a baking tray and bake for 6–8 minutes or until crisp and golden brown. Allow to cool.

Scatter the chopped pumpkin on a baking tray, drizzle with the olive oil and season with salt and pepper. Bake for 10–15 minutes or until tender.

Meanwhile, put the pancetta in a heavy-based frying pan and cook over a medium heat until crisp. Drain on kitchen paper.

Spoon the pumpkin on to the crostini, sprinkle with the pancetta and arrange some Parmesan shavings on top. Serve immediately.

tempura onion rings

Serves 10

2 large Spanish onions

sea salt and pepper

3–4 tbsp flour to dust

groundnut oil to deep-fry

Batter:

80g self-raising flour

1 small free-range egg yolk

2 free-range egg whites

paprika to dust (optional)

Slice the onions finely and place in a bowl. Season with salt and pepper and add 3–4 tbsp flour. Toss the onion slices to coat in the flour.

To make the batter, sift the flour into a bowl and make a well in the middle. Add the egg yolk, then gradually beat in 150ml cold water to make a smooth batter. In another bowl, whisk the egg whites until softly peaking, then fold into the batter.

Heat the oil for deep-frying in a suitable pan to 180°C. Have ready a baking tray lined with kitchen paper.

Deep-fry the onion rings in batches. One by one, dip into the batter and then transfer to the hot oil, using a pair of tongs. Fry for 3–4 minutes until crisp and golden in colour. Transfer to the paper-lined tray to drain and keep warm while you cook the rest.

Serve the onion rings as soon as they are all cooked, dusted with a little paprika if you like.

pan-fried baby octopus

Serves 10

500g cleaned baby octopus
100g plain flour
sea salt and pepper
olive oil to fry
lemon or lime wedges to serve

Cut the octopus into 3cm pieces. Put the flour into a large plastic bag and season generously. Add the octopus and toss around to coat thoroughly with seasoned flour. Have ready a baking tray lined with kitchen paper.

Heat a 2.5cm depth of olive oil in a small, deep frying pan. When hot, fry the octopus in small batches for 2–3 minutes until crisp and golden. Transfer to the paper-lined tray to drain and keep warm while you cook the rest.

Serve the deep-fried octopus as soon as it is all cooked, with lemon or lime wedges.

spring rolls with a soy dip

Makes 20

20g rice noodles

2 spring onions, diced

20g beansprouts

1 carrot, grated

5cm piece mooli, grated

1 tsp fish sauce

sea salt and pepper

130g packet dried spring roll
  wrappers

groundnut oil to deep-fry

Dipping sauce:

50ml soy sauce mixed with
  1 tsp wasabi

Soak the noodles in boiling water for 3–4 minutes.
Drain and mix with the spring onions, beansprouts,
carrot, mooli, fish sauce and seasoning to taste.

Plunge the wrappers into hand-hot water for
15 seconds until pliable, then lay on a clean surface.
Put a spoonful of the mixture in the centre of each,
fold in the sides and carefully roll up to secure.

Heat the oil in a suitable pan to 180°C. Deep-fry the
spring rolls, a few at a time, for 3–4 minutes until
crisp and golden. Drain on kitchen paper and serve
hot, with the dipping sauce.

"Dried spring roll wrappers are available from supermarkets and Asian food stores. Vary the filling as you like – try prawns, chicken or duck – but don't overfill them or they will split"

king prawns in breadcrumbs

Makes 20

20 raw tiger prawns, peeled and deveined (with tail shell left on)

1 free-range egg white, beaten

125g fresh white breadcrumbs

groundnut oil to deep-fry

Hold each tiger prawn by the tail end and dip first into the egg white and then into the breadcrumbs. Gently shake off excess crumbs and place on a baking tray lined with greaseproof paper while you coat the rest.

Heat the oil for deep-frying in a suitable pan to 180°C. Deep-fry the prawns in small batches. Drop them into the hot oil, one at a time, and cook for 3–4 minutes or until they just turn pink. Drain well on kitchen paper. Serve warm.

"I love courgette flowers, but you can't always find them. Fortunately fine courgette slices – cut lengthways using a mandolin – work equally well"

wild sea bass
WRAPPED IN COURGETTE FLOWERS

Makes 20

250g wild sea bass fillet, with skin

20 courgette flowers, or thin strips of courgette

olive oil to drizzle

sea salt and pepper

Heat the oven to 200°C/Gas 6. Line a baking tray with greaseproof paper.

Cut the sea bass into small even-sized pieces. Carefully wrap each one in a courgette flower or thin strip of courgette and secure with a wooden cocktail stick or short kebab stick.

Arrange the sea bass parcels on the baking tray and drizzle with a little olive oil. Bake for 4–5 minutes, then leave to rest for a minute or two.

Season the sea bass lightly with salt and pepper, and serve warm.

"I only ever use scallops that have been hand-dived (rather than dredged from the seabed along with grit and sand) and I suggest you do the same"

scallops in parma ham
WITH MONKFISH AND ROSEMARY

Makes 20

10 scallops, shelled and cleaned

10 slices Parma ham

250g monkfish fillet, skinned

2–3 long rosemary sprigs

olive oil to drizzle

Heat the oven to 200°C/Gas 6. Slice the scallops in half horizontally. Cut the Parma ham slices in half lengthways. Cut the monkfish into small chunks. Break the rosemary stems into short twigs.

Wrap each scallop disc in a strip of Parma ham, top with a piece of monkfish and secure with a rosemary twig or two.

Carefully transfer to a baking tray and drizzle with a little olive oil. Roast in the oven for 3–4 minutes until just firm to the touch.

Allow to stand for a few minutes, then serve warm.

seared tuna with herbs

Makes 20

250g tuna fillet (mid-loin cut), in a squared log,
  about 10cm long and 3cm across
pepper
1 tbsp olive oil
4 tbsp chopped parsley
4 tbsp chopped chervil

Trim the tuna if necessary and season with pepper. Brush a 20cm square of foil with olive oil and scatter the herbs across the centre. Lay the tuna log on the herbs, then roll to coat on all sides.

Roll the herb-coated tuna in the foil very tightly and twist the ends to seal (like a Christmas cracker). Roll the tuna roll back and forth on the work surface to round off the squared edges. Refrigerate for 20 minutes.

Heat a cast-iron frying pan over a high heat, then put the foil parcel in the pan and cook quickly for about 15–20 seconds on each side. Remove the foil parcel and allow to cool.

Place the foil-wrapped tuna in the fridge and leave to firm up for at least 30 minutes, or up to 4 hours.

To serve, unwrap the tuna and cut into thin slices with a very sharp knife. Serve immediately.

"As this dish is served raw, only very fresh, sushi-grade tuna is suitable. Ask your fishmonger to prepare this for you"

steak tartare

"Prime fillet of beef is the key to this recipe and it is worth having it freshly minced by your butcher. Alternatively, this can be done in the food processor, but take care not to overwork"

Serves 10

250g minced fillet steak

1 tbsp minced red onion

1 tbsp finely chopped flat-leaf parsley

2 tsp Dijon mustard

freshly ground black pepper

1 free-range egg yolk

2 vine-ripened tomatoes, to serve

Put the minced steak into a bowl with the onion, parsley and mustard. Mix well, seasoning with pepper to taste, then bind the mixture with the egg yolk.

Immerse the tomatoes in boiling water for 20 seconds or so, then remove and peel off the skins. Halve the tomatoes, scoop out the seeds, then cut the flesh into small dice.

Serve small portions of the steak tartare on teaspoons, topped with the tomato dice.

pork satay
IN LETTUCE WITH PEANUT DIPPING SAUCE

Makes 10

1 pork fillet (tenderloin)

100ml soy sauce

25ml dry sherry

2 star anise

1 tsp coriander seeds

1 tsp grated fresh root
   ginger

2 tsp thin honey

oil to brush

Peanut dipping sauce:

1 tbsp sugar

100g unsalted peanuts

sea salt and pepper

To assemble:

1 round lettuce, separated
   into leaves

2 spring onions, finely sliced

handful of coriander leaves

Cut the pork into bite-sized pieces and put into a bowl. Add the soy sauce, sherry, star anise, coriander seeds, ginger and honey, and toss to coat the pork in the mixture. Leave to marinate for 2 hours.

To make the dipping sauce, dissolve the sugar in 125ml water in a small saucepan and bring to the boil. Add the peanuts and take off the heat. Whiz the mixture in a blender or food processor until fairly smooth. Season with salt and pepper to taste.

Heat a cast-iron griddle pan until very hot and brush with oil. Add the pork and cook quickly for 2–3 minutes, turning until golden brown on both sides and cooked through.

Place 2 or 3 pieces of pork in the centre of a lettuce leaf and scatter with a little spring onion and a few coriander leaves. Roll up and secure with a cocktail stick. Repeat with the rest of the pork.

Serve the pork satay warm, with the peanut dipping sauce.

bellini

Serves 2

60ml peach juice

200ml Champagne or
  Prosecco (sparkling wine)

Pour the peach juice into chilled flute glasses, top with the Champagne or Prosecco and serve.

strawberry champagne cocktail

Serves 2

60ml strawberry purée

200ml Champagne or
  sparkling wine

halved strawberry to finish

Pour the strawberry purée into chilled flute glasses, top with the Champagne or sparkling wine and decorate with the strawberry halves.

champagne alexander

Serves 2

2 sugar cubes

40ml brandy

200ml Champagne

Place a sugar cube in each of two flute glasses, add the brandy and top up with the Champagne.

pina colada

Serves 2

8 ice cubes

few drops of Angostura
    bitters

100ml pineapple juice

100ml white rum

150ml soda water

Place the ice cubes in tall glasses, add the Angostura bitters, and pour on the pineapple juice and rum. Stir thoroughly. Top up with the soda water, stir once and serve.

bloody mary

Serves 4

12 ice cubes

200ml vodka

600ml tomato juice

4 dashes of Worcestershire
    sauce

4 dashes of Tabasco

4 celery sticks

pinch of celery salt

Place the ice cubes in tall glasses, add the vodka and then top up with the tomato juice. Add a dash each of Worcestershire sauce and Tabasco to each glass, Pop in a celery stick, sprinkle with a little celery salt and serve.

"Champagne is so evocative of luxury, celebration and fun. Nothing can be easier than popping open a few bottles and making a few simple cocktails – it's the easiest way to get a party off to a great start"

posh

It's rewarding to create dishes that are a bit more special at home, and I think you will find plenty of inspiration here. Lobster thermidor is far easier than you might imagine, or for an impressive, inexpensive dish, try my pork fillet in prosciutto. Posh food that isn't time-consuming is the essence of this chapter. It's the kind of food Tana likes to cook, but her problem is that she never really knows when I'm likely to turn up for dinner. These recipes are ideal – simple to prepare and quick to finish.

frisée and potato soup WITH TARRAGON

Serves 6

300g potatoes, peeled

1 leek, white part only, well washed

400ml chicken stock

1/2 tsp coriander seeds, or to taste, freshly ground

1 head of frisée, stem removed

sea salt and pepper

handful of tarragon leaves

120ml double cream

large knob of unsalted butter

Dice the potatoes and leek and put in a pan with the stock and coriander seeds. Bring to the boil, then simmer for 10–15 minutes until the potato is just tender. Strain through a chinois into a clean pan. Set aside half the leek and potato for later; add the rest to the pan. Slowly bring to a simmer.

Take the pale centre leaves from the frisée, roll them together and shred very finely with a sharp knife to make a chiffonade. Set aside for the garnish.

Tear up the remaining frisée and add to the soup. Season, then add the tarragon and cook until just wilted – no longer or you will lose the colour. Immediately pour into a blender or food processor and whiz to a purée. Strain through the chinois back into the clean pan. Stir in the cream and heat through. Check the seasoning.

Meanwhile, heat the butter in a small frying pan, add the reserved potato and leek and cook over a high heat to colour lightly.

Pile the sautéed leek and potato into the centre of warm soup plates, pour the soup around and top with the frisée chiffonade. Serve at once.

turnip soup
WITH LANGOUSTINES AND MANGO

Serves 6

900g turnips, pceled

large knob of butter

1 onion, chopped

450ml chicken stock

125ml double cream

sea salt and pepper

Mango garnish:

1 ripe, firm mango, peeled,
   sliced or diced and pitted

knob of butter (optional)

2 tsp sugar (optional)

Saffron langoustines:

1–2 tbsp olive oil

1 garlic clove, crushed

pinch of saffron threads

18–30 langoustines or tiger
   prawns (or more), blanched
   for 1 minute and peeled

To finish:

handful of sorrel leaves,
   shredded (optional)

olive oil to drizzle

Roughly chop the turnips. Melt the butter in a medium pan, add the onion and sweat for a few minutes to soften. Add the turnips and stock and bring to a simmer. Cook gently for 20–30 minutes until the turnip is very soft.

Caramelise the mango in the meantime if you like. Melt a knob of butter with the sugar in a heavy-based frying pan and cook to a light caramel. Add the mango and cook for a few minutes until lightly tinged brown. Remove and set aside.

Pass the soup mixture through a mouli. Return to the pan, add the cream and check the seasoning. Allow to simmer very gently while you cook the langoustines.

Heat the olive oil in a small frying pan, and add the garlic, saffron and langoustines. Sauté quickly for a minute or two on each side; do not overcook.

Pour the soup into warm soup plates and arrange the mango in the centre. Top with a little shredded sorrel if using. Arrange the langoustines around the mango and drizzle with a little olive oil. Serve immediately.

turnip
soup

"I love the heat and flavour of turnip and consider it to be a very underrated vegetable. I often use it to thicken soups in place of potato. Here turnip comes into its own, marrying perfectly with the sweetness of caramelised mango and plump, juicy langoustines"

carpaccio of beef
WITH ROCKET AND PARMESAN

Serves 6 as a starter

olive oil to brush

2–3 tbsp black
   peppercorns, freshly
   crushed

500g piece fillet of beef,
   well-trimmed

2 tbsp chopped flat-leaf
   parsley

Dressing:

1 tsp thin honey, warmed

juice of ½ lemon

1 tbsp white wine vinegar

1 tsp wholegrain mustard

150ml olive oil

To serve:

handful of rocket leaves

freshly shaved Parmesan

Brush a large piece of foil with a little olive oil and scatter the crushed peppercorns in the centre. Roll the beef fillet in the pepper to coat completely. Wrap the fillet in the foil and secure the ends tightly. Rest in the fridge for 30 minutes.

Place a heavy-based frying pan over a high heat and sear the foil packet for 20–30 seconds on each of the four sides. Allow to cool, then return to the fridge for at least 1 hour.

For the dressing, put the honey into a bowl and whisk in the lemon juice, wine vinegar and mustard, followed by the olive oil.

Unwrap the beef and roll in the chopped parsley, then cut into very thin slices, using a razor-sharp knife.

Toss the rocket in the dressing and arrange on individual plates. Pile the rocket into the centre and scatter the Parmesan shavings over. Serve at once.

"Classic carpaccio is finely sliced raw beef served with a light mayonnaise or dressing. I like to sear the outside of the fillet very briefly, which gives it an almost smoky finish, but you can omit this stage if you like"

lobster thermidor

Serves 6

3 live medium lobsters

250ml fish stock (preferably lobster stock)

250ml dry white wine

splash of Noilly Prat

250ml double cream

1 tsp Dijon mustard

sea salt and pepper

2 tbsp freshly grated Parmesan

First, put the lobsters in the freezer for about 30 minutes to make them sleepy. When ready to cook, make sure you kill them quickly: Lay stomach downwards and plunge the tip of a knife through the crossmark on the skull, then cut the head in half. (If you prefer you can plunge them into a pan of boiling water for 2 minutes.)

Split each lobster in half lengthways through the tail shell and twist off the claws; reserve the empty half-shells. Discard the head and carefully remove the meat from the tail shells, discarding the entrails. Wash the reserved tail shells. Crack open the claws with a nutcracker and extract the meat. Place the reserved tail shells on a large baking tray and pile the lobster meat into them.

Boil the stock and wine in a pan until reduced by half. Add the Noilly Prat and cream and let bubble until reduced to a sauce-like consistency. Stir in the mustard and adjust the seasoning.

Heat the grill to high. Carefully spoon the sauce over the lobster meat and scatter the Parmesan on top. Place the lobsters under the grill and cook for 2–3 minutes until the sauce is bubbly and golden brown. Serve immediately, with a green salad.

"Ready-cooked lobsters are never as good as those you cook yourself, so I recommend you get to grips with handling a live lobster! Their claws will be wrapped in thick bands so they won't nip you. With a ready-cooked lobster you might end up with a dry, rubbery texture rather than deliciously succulent meat"

Serves 6

1kg fresh razor clams or
   medium clams
300ml dry white wine
200ml fish stock or water
2 shallots, very finely diced
1 tbsp chopped tarragon
15g butter
300g girolles (golden
   chanterelles), trimmed
   and cleaned
50ml double cream
sea salt and pepper
2 tbsp chopped flat-leaf
   parsley

razor clams with girolles

To clean the clams, put them in a large bowl of cold water, leave for 5 minutes, then drain. Repeat twice more, replacing with fresh water each time. Pull away the beards and scrub the shells to remove any barnacles. Discard any open clams.

Pour the wine and stock into a very large pan. Add the shallots and tarragon and bring to the boil. Add the clams, cover with a tight-fitting lid and cook for 3–4 minutes to steam them open, shaking the pan twice. Drain in a colander over another pan to save the stock. Keep the clams warm in the colander over the hot stock, covering them with the pan lid. Discard any that do not open.

Melt the butter in a pan and sauté the mushrooms for 2–3 minutes. Add 200ml reserved stock and bring to a simmer. Stir in the cream, season and heat through.

Divide the clams between warm bowls, spoon over the mushroom sauce and sprinkle with chopped parsley.

> "Confit is an old technique, once used to preserve meat such as duck. To 'confit' you simply poach the food in warm oil or fat, sealing in all the delicious natural flavours"

confit of trout
WITH SAUCE MOUSSELINE

Serves 6

6 large trout fillets, with skin

sea salt

500ml olive oil for cooking

3 small ripe avocados

large handful of rocket leaves

Sauce mousseline:

125ml double cream

125ml mayonnaise

3 tbsp lemon juice

sea salt and pepper

Check the trout fillets for small bones and remove any you find with tweezers. Scatter plenty of sea sea over the trout and leave to stand for 30 minutes. Rinse the trout and place in a dish of cold water. Leave to soak for 20 minutes, then drain and pat dry.

Heat the olive oil in a deep frying pan to 50°C (warm enough to cook the fish and cool enough to be able to place your finger in the oil without it burning). Place the trout in the oil and maintain the temperature for 10 minutes. Remove the fillets with a slotted spoon and allow to cool.

For the sauce mousseline, whip the cream until softly peaking, then fold in the mayonnaise and lemon juice. Season with salt and pepper to taste.

Halve and pit the avocados, then slice lengthways and arrange on serving plates. Flake the confit trout, arrange next to the avocado and spoon over a little sauce mousseline. Garnish with rocket and serve.

halibut bourguignon

Serves 6

125g shallots (unpeeled)

400ml red wine

125g bacon lardons

4 tbsp olive oil

6 garlic cloves (unpeeled)

125g button mushrooms

50g butter

6 halibut fillets, about 150g
each, skinned

250g spinach leaves, well
washed

sea salt

Blanch the shallots in boiling water for 2 minutes, then drain and peel. Meanwhile, boil the red wine in a pan to reduce by half.

Sauté the lardons in a heavy-based frying pan until crisp. Remove and set aside.

Add 2 tbsp olive oil to the frying pan and heat. Add the shallots, garlic and mushrooms and sauté until softened and the shallots are lightly caramelised. Stir in the bacon; keep warm.

Meanwhile, heat the butter and remaining oil in a large frying pan until foaming. Pan-fry the halibut fillets for 2–3 minutes on each side until just cooked. Remove to a warm plate and rest for a few minutes.

Cook the spinach in a large pan over a medium heat, with a little water and a pinch of salt, until just wilted. Drain well.

Pile the spinach into the centre of warm plates and place the fish on top. Spoon over the mushrooms, shallots, garlic and bacon. Add the reduced red wine to the shallot pan, stirring to deglaze, then drizzle over the fish and vegetables. Serve with new potatoes.

halibut bourguignon

"Other firm fish fillets, such as cod, brill or turbot can be cooked in this way. Cooking time may vary slightly, according to the thickness of the fish"

"The secret of cooking fish is mastering the 'cuisson' or the point at which it is ready but not overcooked. Fish firms up during cooking and, when it has reached 'cuisson', it will feel firm but give slightly if you press the flesh gently with your index finger"

bacon-wrapped chicken legs
STUFFED WITH PORK AND PISTACHIOS

Serves 6

6 boned-out medium
   chicken drumsticks or
   thighs

sea salt and pepper

24 rashers rindless streaky
   bacon (approximately)

3 tbsp olive oil

1 tbsp sherry vinegar

2 tbsp Marsala

ladleful of brown chicken
   stock

Stuffing:

350g good-quality pork
   sausage meat

handful of skinned pistachio
   nuts, roughly chopped

1 egg yolk

4 thyme sprigs, leaves
   stripped and chopped

To make the stuffing, mix the sausage meat with the pistachio nuts, egg yolk and thyme. Season well with salt and pepper.

Open out the chicken legs or thighs, season with pepper and divide the stuffing between them. Roll up to enclose. Lay about 4 bacon rashers on a board, overlapping them slightly. Put one stuffed chicken portion on top and wrap the bacon around to cover completely. Repeat with the rest of the chicken.

Cut 6 very large pieces of foil. Wrap each chicken parcel tightly in foil, twisting the ends to seal. Roll back and forth to even the shape.

Poach the chicken parcels, two or three at a time, in a large pan of boiling water for about 20 minutes, depending on size. Allow to cool completely, then remove the foil.

Heat the olive oil in a large frying pan and sauté the chicken parcels until the bacon is brown and crisp on all sides and the parcels are cooked through. Transfer to a warm platter and rest in a warm place.

Deglaze the pan with the sherry vinegar, then add the Marsala and stock. Let bubble to reduce by half, then skim off excess fat and check the seasoning.

Cut the chicken into thick slices and arrange on warm plates. Spoon over the jus and serve with rice.

"Speciality free-range chickens are probably one of the most exciting things I have featured on my menus this year. Quality birds, such as Label Anglaise, are bred for the size of breast and quality of flavour. They taste nothing like battery-farmed chickens"

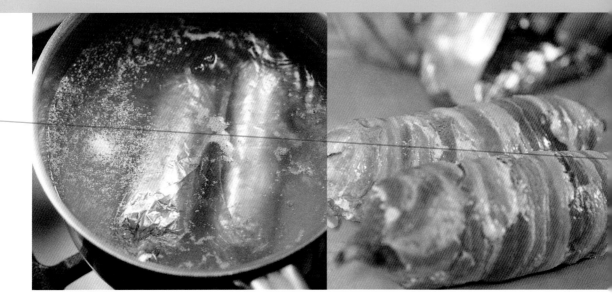

bacon-wrapped chicken legs

guinea fowl with broad beans
GEM LETTUCE AND BACON

Serves 6

6 boneless guinea fowl
   breasts, about 175g each
300ml chicken stock
150ml double cream
sea salt and pepper
300g podded broad beans
150g bacon lardons
3 tbsp olive oil
75g unsalted butter, diced
3 Little Gem lettuces,
   quartered lengthways

"Poaching the guinea fowl breasts in cling film seals in all the flavours. If you don't like the idea, then poach them directly in chicken stock"

Wrap each guinea fowl breast tightly in food-safe cling film, twisting the ends to seal. Immerse in a pan of boiling water and poach for 5 minutes, Remove from the water and let cool, then chill for 30 minutes.

Boil the stock in a pan to reduce by half, then add the cream and let bubble until reduced by half again to make a creamy sauce. Season to taste.

Blanch the broad beans in boiling water for 2–3 minutes, then drain and refresh in a bowl of iced water. Slip the beans out of their tough outer skins.

Sauté the lardons in a heavy-based frying pan until crisp. Drain on kitchen paper and keep warm.

Heat the olive oil in the frying pan. Unwrap the guinea fowl and pan-fry skin-side down for 5 minutes. Turn and cook for a further 3 minutes. Remove from the pan and rest in a warm place for 5 minutes.

Over a low heat, gradually whisk the butter into the sauce, then bring back to a simmer and check the seasoning. Add the lettuce and broad beans and cook for 2 minutes or until the lettuce starts to wilt.

Slice each guinea fowl breast lengthways into three. Spoon the wilted lettuce and broad beans on to warm plates, using a slotted spoon. Place the guinea fowl breasts on top and scatter over the bacon. Spoon the sauce over the guinea fowl and serve.

oven-roast duck breast
WITH CARAMELISED SWEDE

Serves 6

6 Gressingham duck
breasts, about 175g each

1 or 2 knobs of butter

handful of thyme sprigs

good splash of red wine

2 large ladlefuls brown
chicken stock

sea salt and pepper

Caramelised swede:

1 large or 2 small swede,
peeled

40g butter

2cm knob of fresh root
ginger, peeled and grated

1–2 tsp thin honey

Heat the oven to 200°C/Gas 6. With a sharp knife, score the duck breast skin in a criss-cross pattern, taking care to avoid cutting through to the meat.

Cut the swede into cubes, roughly 2.5cm, and simmer in salted water to cover for 10 minutes or until barely tender, then drain thoroughly.

Heat a heavy-based frying pan over a high heat. Add the duck breasts, skin-side down, and sear for a few minutes, pressing down on the flesh to ensure an even colour. Turn the duck breasts over, add a knob of butter with the thyme sprigs, and cook for 30 seconds only. Transfer to a roasting pan, adding the thyme, too. You may need to do this in batches.

Roast the duck breasts in the oven for 8–10 minutes, then transfer to a warm plate and rest in a warm place for 10 minutes. Put the roasting pan over a medium heat and add the wine, stirring to deglaze. Pour in the stock, bring to the boil and skim. Let bubble until reduced by half. Check the seasoning.

Caramelise the swede, meanwhile. Heat the butter in a pan, add the swede with the ginger and honey, and sauté for 3–4 minutes until lightly caramelised.

Pile the swede into the centre of warm plates. Thickly slice the duck breasts and arrange on top of the swede. Spoon over the jus and serve with fondant potatoes (page 190) if you like.

"The secret of perfectly cooked duck breasts is to cook them quickly and rest them well before carving. The skin should be crisp and golden brown and the meat pink and succulent"

oven-roast duck breast

pork fillet in prosciutto
WITH BAKED COUSCOUS

Serves 6

80g prosciutto slices

2 pork fillets (tenderloins), about 350g each, well trimmed

sea salt and pepper

2–3 tbsp olive oil, plus extra to oil

4 thyme sprigs, leaves stripped

250g couscous

40g Parmesan, freshly grated

handful of flat-leaf parsley, finely chopped

knob of soft unsalted butter

splash of Marsala

ladleful of brown chicken stock

Lay half the prosciutto slices on a board, overlapping them slightly, then lay one pork fillet across at one end. Wrap the pork in the prosciutto and season with pepper. Repeat with the other fillet.

Cut two 40 x 30cm sheets of foil, drizzle a little olive oil down the centre and sprinkle with the thyme leaves. Place the pork fillet on top, bring the edges of the foil up and fold together over the pork, then roll to enclose, twisting the ends to seal. Rest in the fridge for 15 minutes. Heat the oven to 200°C/Gas 6.

Put the couscous in a bowl, pour on 400ml boiling water, cover and leave to stand for 10 minutes. Add the Parmesan and parsley, fork through and season liberally. Place 6 large individual ring moulds on a baking tray, brush with butter and then oil. Spoon in the couscous and press down with the back of the spoon.

Place the pork parcels on another baking tray and bake for 15–20 minutes, depending on the thickness of the fillets. Take the pork out of the oven and then bake the couscous cakes for 10 minutes.

Heat 2–3 tbsp olive oil in a large frying pan. Remove the foil from the pork parcels, reserving any juices. Add the prosciutto-wrapped pork fillets to the pan and pan-fry for about 10 minutes, turning until the prosciutto is crisp and brown all over. Remove to a warm plate and rest in a warm place.

Add the Marsala to the frying pan with the reserved pork juices, stirring to deglaze. Add the stock and boil until reduced by half. Check the seasoning.

Cut the pork into thick slices. Unmould a couscous cake on to the centre of each warm plate, pressing it out with the back of a spoon. Surround with the pork and spoon over the jus. Serve with a green vegetable or salad.

"The beauty of this dish is that it can be prepared ahead – ready to bake when you're ready to eat. The couscous cakes simply rest in the oven while you finish the pork"

aubergine gâteau
WITH CHERRY TOMATOES, BASIL AND PARMESAN

Serves 6

2 medium aubergines,
   thinly sliced
olive oil to drizzle
large knob of unsalted
   butter
600g cherry tomatoes,
   halved
1 garlic clove, crushed
handful of basil leaves
sea salt and pepper
75g Parmesan, freshly
   grated

Heat the oven to 200°C/Gas 6. Thinly slice the aubergines and lay the slices out on two large oiled baking sheets. Drizzle with olive oil and bake for 5–8 minutes until softened and lightly browned.

Line a 20cm round cake tin with greaseproof paper. Melt the butter in a large sauté pan and cook the cherry tomatoes with the garlic until soft and pulpy. Tear in the basil leaves and season with salt and pepper.

Layer a third of the aubergine slices over the base of the prepared tin, top with half the tomato mixture, then scatter over some Parmesan. Add another layer of aubergine, then the remaining tomato mixture. Cover with a final layer of aubergine and then sprinkle generously with Parmesan.

Bake the gâteau for 10 minutes until the topping is golden and bubbling. Allow to stand for 5 minutes, then turn out on to a warm plate. Cut into wedges and serve with crusty bread.

"Contrary to popular belief, I'm more than happy to cook for vegetarians. Fortunately, this stunning dish is equally appealing to carnivores like me"

fondant potatoes

Serves 6

1kg floury potatoes, such as Maris Piper

1 litre chicken stock

75–100g salted butter

4–5 garlic cloves (unpeeled)

1 or 2 thyme sprigs

1 rosemary sprig

sea salt and pepper

"readily and fries at a higher heat so the food caramelises very
the flavour. This is one instance where it is quite acceptable to use
an integral part of the dish"

Peel the potatoes and cut into chunky slices, about 2–3cm thick. Place in a
pan with the stock and bring to the boil. Turn down the heat and simmer for
10–12 minutes until tender when pierced with a knife but still quite firm and not
breaking up. Drain well (saving the stock for a soup or sauce).

Heat the butter in a heavy-based frying pan until it starts to foam. Add the
potatoes, cut-side down, with the garlic and herbs. Cook for 4–5 minutes, then turn
and cook for a further 3–4 minutes or until the potatoes are golden in colour.
Discard the garlic and herbs, season with salt and pepper and serve.

Serves 6

10 ripe passion fruit

6 large free-range egg yolks

75g caster sugar

25ml vodka (optional)

350ml double cream

passion fruit parfait

Halve 8 passion fruit and scoop out the pulp and seeds into a blender or food processor. Whiz thoroughly, then tip into a small pan and boil until reduced by half, to 60–70ml. Rub through a sieve into a bowl and set aside to cool.

Whisk the egg yolks in a medium heatproof bowl until smooth and fluffy, then set the bowl over a pan of very hot water and continue to whisk until doubled in volume, pale and stiff. Take the pan off the heat.

Dissolve the sugar in 50ml water in a small heavy-based pan over a low heat, stirring. Then stop stirring and boil until the temperature registers 110°C on a sugar thermometer.

Return the bowl of whisked yolks set over the pan to a low heat. Slowly add the sugar syrup, whisking constantly until the mixture is thick, glossy and mousse-like. Take the bowl off the pan and whisk off the heat for 5 minutes or until cooled. Fold in the passion fruit purée, and the vodka if using, then chill for 1 hour.

Whip the cream until softly peaking, then carefully fold into the passion fruit mixture. Pour into 6 individual moulds, such as darioles, or ring moulds set on a tray. Freeze for 12 hours, or overnight.

To turn out, wipe a hot cloth around the moulds (or dip darioles into hot water for a second or two). Unmould the parfaits on to plates and spoon on a little passion fruit pulp to serve.

chocolate pots
WITH GRAND MARNIER

Serves 6

200g good-quality dark
   chocolate (about 60%
   cocoa solids)
6 free-range eggs, separated
50ml Grand Marnier

Melt the chocolate in a heatproof bowl set over a pan of gently simmering water – take care to avoid overheating otherwise it will seize. Remove the bowl from the pan and cool, almost to room temperature.

Whisk the egg whites in a clean, grease-free bowl until softly peaking.

Beat the egg yolks into the melted chocolate, then stir in the Grand Marnier. Carefully fold in the whisked egg whites. Pour into 6 custard pots and chill for 3 hours before serving.

lime pannacotta

INFUSED WITH MINT AND TEQUILA

Serves 6

600ml double cream

150ml milk

8 mint leaves

4–5 sheets leaf gelatine

60g caster sugar

finely grated zest of 3 limes

$1\frac{1}{2}$ tbsp tequila

lime segments to decorate

Pour the cream and milk into a small saucepan, add the mint leaves and bring to a simmer. Let bubble for 5 minutes to reduce by about a third.

Meanwhile, soak the gelatine sheets in a bowl of cold water to soften for about 5 minutes.

Strain the boiling cream mixture into a bowl and stir in the sugar, lime zest and tequila. Take the gelatine leaves, gently squeeze out excess water, then add to the hot cream mixture and stir until dissolved.

Pour the mixture into 6 dariole moulds and allow to cool, then refrigerate the pannacottas for 2–3 hours or until set.

To turn out, gently tease the side of each pannacotta away from the mould, then invert on to a plate and shake to release. Arrange a few lime segments on each plate and serve.

dinner for
two

We should all make time in our lives for romance. Tana and I try to keep to this philosophy – it's dinner after the children are tucked up in bed, either at home or in a restaurant. Food is sensual and sharing a meal is so romantic. Slaving over a hot stove trying to master a tricky dish, however, isn't at all romantic. There's a reason why oysters and Champagne have long been the food of lovers. Try my oysters rockefeller for a twist on the classic, and follow with rump of lamb with a rosemary-scented jus … divine.

oysters rockefeller

Serves 2

12 oysters

100g unsalted butter

1 small celery stick, finely
  sliced

1 slice of fennel, chopped

2 spring onions, finely sliced

1 garlic clove, finely
  chopped

1 tbsp chopped parsley

handful of watercress leaves

few drops of Tabasco, or to
  taste

dash of Pernod

2 slices white bread, crusts
  removed

lemon wedges to serve

Shuck the oysters (see below). Place them in their half-shells on a baking tray and set aside. Heat the grill to high.

Melt the butter in a sauté pan until foaming. Add the celery, fennel, spring onions and garlic, and cook for 2 minutes, then add the parsley and watercress and cook for 30 seconds.

Tip into a blender or food processor, add the Tabasco, Pernod and bread and whiz for about 30 seconds until you have 'green breadcrumbs'.

Spoon the crumb mixture on top of the oysters to cover them completely. Grill for 30 seconds or until the topping begins to colour.

Arrange the oysters on plates, add the lemon wedges and serve immediately.

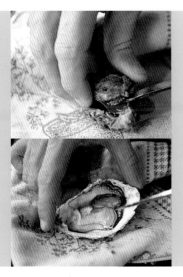

"To shuck oysters hold rounded-side down in a cloth. Insert an oyster knife into the hinge and twist from side to side to sever the muscle and lift the top shell. Tip juices into a bowl. Slide knife under oyster to release it. Rinse oysters in their juice, check for shell fragments and return to lower shells"

clam soup with samphire

Serves 2

12 fresh medium clams,
  cleaned (see page 172)
75ml dry white wine
50g pancetta, diced
25g unsalted butter
1 onion, finely chopped
350ml fish stock
2 potatoes, peeled and cut
  into 1cm dice
2 thyme sprigs, leaves only
sea salt and pepper
large handful of samphire
100ml double cream
2 tbsp chopped flat-leaf
  parsley

Put the clams into a large pan, add the wine and 75ml water and bring to the boil. Cover with a tight-fitting lid and cook for 2–3 minutes to steam the clams open. Drain, reserving the liquor. When cool enough to handle, shell the clams, chop roughly and set aside.

Cook the pancetta in a dry pan over a medium heat until the fat starts to run, then increase the heat slightly and cook until crisp; remove and set aside.

Add the butter to the pan and sweat the onion over a low heat until soft and translucent. Gradually stir in the stock, then add the potatoes, thyme leaves and pepper. Simmer for 10–15 minutes until the potatoes are tender.

Ladle about a third of the stock and potatoes into a blender or food processor and whiz to a purée. Stir back into the soup to thicken it slightly.

Add the clams and samphire. Cook for a few minutes, then stir in the cream and pancetta. Heat through, stirring, and adjust the seasoning. Serve in warm bowls, sprinkled with the chopped parsley.

"Clams are not used enough in this country. They have a great meaty texture, which is particularly good in soups, such as this chowder"

steamed asparagus
WITH ORANGE HOLLANDAISE

Serves 2

1 bunch medium asparagus,
   trimmed

Orange hollandaise:

juice of 2 oranges,
   preferably blood oranges

70g unsalted butter

1 free-range egg yolk

sea salt

pinch of cayenne pepper

squeeze of lemon juice

To prepare the asparagus, break off the tough ends and peel the lower part of the stalks thinly, using a potato peeler.

To make the hollandaise, boil the orange juice in a small pan until reduced by half, then remove from the heat and allow to cool. Melt the butter in another pan and cool until tepid.

Put the egg yolk into a small bowl and whisk in 1 tbsp water. Set the bowl over a pan of hot water and slowly whisk in the orange juice – the sauce will thicken as you whisk.

Take the bowl off the heat and whisk for a few more minutes, then slowly trickle in the butter as you continue to whisk. Don't add the butter too quickly or the sauce will curdle. When all the butter has been incorporated, the sauce should be thick. Season with salt and cayenne, and add a little lemon juice to taste.

Steam the asparagus in the meantime for about 3–4 minutes until tender. (If you don't have a steamer, cook the asparagus upright in a tall covered pan about one-third filled with boiling water, so the tips cook in the steam.)

Drain the asparagus and serve at once, with the orange hollandaise.

"An orange hollandaise makes a great dipping sauce for freshly steamed asparagus spears. Blood oranges lend a superb flavour and colour to this sauce, so look out for them during their short season. Otherwise use the sweetest, fullest-flavoured oranges you can find"

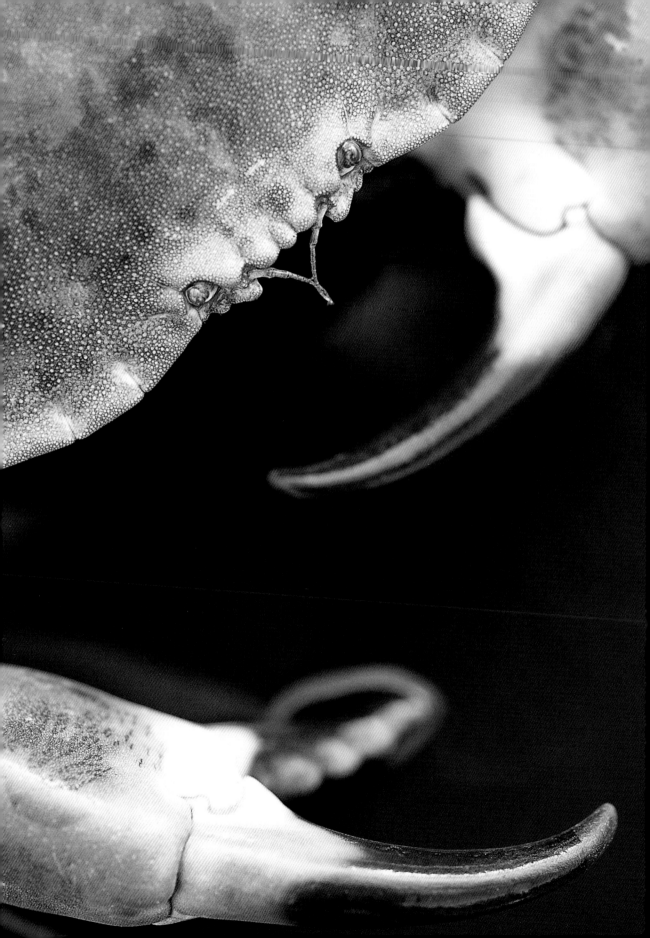

crab salad

WITH PASSION FRUIT DRESSING

Serves 2

200g fresh white crabmeat

125g salad leaves, such as
    rocket, watercress and
    radicchio

100g yellow or red cherry
    tomatoes, halved

2 passion fruit, halved

2 tbsp classic vinaigrette

Check that the crabmeat is free from fragments of shell. Arrange the salad leaves and tomatoes on individual serving plates.

Pile the crabmeat into the centre – using a ring mould to shape a neat cylinder if you like.

Scoop out the passion fruit pulp and seeds, and whisk into the vinaigrette. Drizzle over the salad leaves and serve.

tiger prawn salad
WITH MANGO AND AVOCADO

Devein the prawns if necessary. Whiz half the mango flesh in a blender or small food processor to a purée; set aside. Dice the rest of the mango.

Halve and slice the avocado, removing the stone. Arrange the slices around the outside of a small platter and drizzle over the lemon juice.

Heat the olive oil in a frying pan, add the ginger and garlic and cook for 30 seconds. Add the prawns and stir-fry for 2–3 minutes until they turn pink – don't overcook. Drizzle with the lime juice and take off the heat. Discard the ginger and garlic.

Add the diced mango to the prawns and toss together. Season with salt and pepper to taste.

Pile the prawns and mango into the middle of the platter and scatter over the parsley. Drizzle the mango purée around the edge of the plate and serve.

Serves 2

12 raw tiger prawns, peeled
  (heads removed)
1 large ripe mango, peeled
1 large ripe avocado, peeled
juice of ½ lemon
1 tbsp olive oil
1cm piece fresh root ginger,
  peeled
1 garlic clove, peeled
juice of 1 lime
sea salt and pepper
1 tbsp chopped flat-leaf
  parsley

"I always look for the largest, freshest tiger prawns in the fish market. They need little cooking and taste divine"

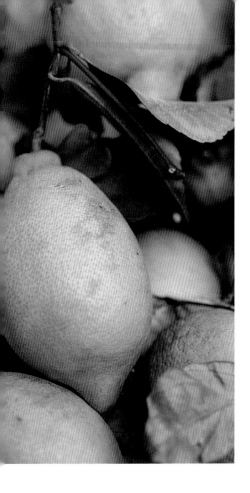

turbot fillets

WITH FENNEL AND LEMON

Serves 2

2 turbot fillets, about 150g each

600ml fish stock

¼ vanilla pod

2 lemongrass stalks

1 tsp coriander seeds

1 fennel bulb, trimmed (fronds reserved)

sea salt and pepper

large knob of butter, plus extra to grease

1 thyme sprig

1 tbsp Pernod

juice of 1 lemon

Check the fish fillets for small bones, then set aside. Put the stock, vanilla, lemongrass and coriander seeds in a large pan. Bring to the boil and boil to reduce by one third. Cool, then strain.

Slice the fennel very finely and blanch in boiling salted water for 2–3 minutes. Drain and refresh in cold water, then drain well.

Heat the oven to 190°C/Gas 5. Lay the fish fillets in a buttered small ovenproof dish. Bring the stock to the boil, pour over the fish and bake for 5 minutes.

Meanwhile, sauté the fennel slices in the butter in a large sauté pan with the thyme until lightly caramelised. Add the Pernod, then the lemon juice. Toss well and season with salt and pepper to taste. Discard the thyme.

Arrange the fennel on warm plates and top with the turbot. Add the fish liquor to the sauté pan, boil to reduce, then drizzle over the fish. Garnish with fennel fronds.

wild sea trout and baby leeks
WITH CRUSHED POTATO AND TOMATO BUTTER

Check the fish fillets for tiny bones, score the skin side deeply and set aside. Cook the potatoes in salted water until tender. Heat the oven to 190°C/Gas 5.

To make the tomato butter sauce, heat the olive oil in a small pan, add the tomatoes and cook over a low heat for 10 minutes. Transfer to a blender or food processor, add the sherry vinegar and sugar and whiz to a purée. Pass through a sieve back into the pan. Add the cream and simmer for a few minutes. Whisk in the butter and basil; keep warm.

Put the tomato halves, cut-side up, on a baking tray, drizzle with a little olive oil and sprinkle with salt. Bake for about 5 minutes (or slowly overnight at 100°C/Gas ¼). Steam the leeks until tender.

Drain the potatoes, toss with a little olive oil over heat, then crush lightly with the back of a fork. Stir in the spring onions and vinaigrette. Season to taste.

To cook the fish, heat a non-stick frying pan and add the olive oil. Fry the fish, skin-side down, for $3\frac{1}{2}$ minutes or until the skin is crisp, then turn and cook for 30 seconds only. Season lightly and rest in the pan for a few minutes.

Pile the crushed potato and leeks in the centre of two warm serving plates and top with the fish fillets. Surround with the cherry tomatoes and serve the tomato butter sauce on the side.

Serves 2

2 wild sea trout or salmon
   fillets, with skin, about
   150g each
250g new potatoes, peeled
sea salt and pepper
125g vine-ripened cherry
   tomatoes, halved
2 tbsp olive oil, plus extra
   to drizzle
125g baby leeks, halved
few spring onions, chopped
2 tbsp classic vinaigrette

tomato butter sauce:

1 tbsp olive oil
125g vine-ripened cherry
   tomatoes
1 tsp sherry vinegar
1 tsp sugar
50ml double cream
25g butter, diced
1 tbsp chopped basil

wild sea trout and baby leeks

"This is a great way to serve fresh wild sea trout or salmon fillets. For best results, cook the fish almost entirely on the skin side, without moving. To make the dish extra special, toss the crushed potatoes with some fresh white crabmeat and chopped coriander"

rump of lamb
WITH ROSEMARY SCENTED JUS

Serves 2

2 lamb rumps, about 200g each

6 tbsp olive oil

1 thyme sprig

3 rosemary sprigs

2 garlic cloves, chopped

sea salt and pepper

1 shallot, thinly sliced

1 baby aubergine, cut into wedges

1 courgette, sliced

$\frac{1}{2}$ red pepper, deseeded and sliced

$\frac{1}{2}$ yellow pepper, deseeded and sliced

1 tbsp sherry vinegar

1 large glass of red wine

Score the skin of the lamb rumps lightly with a sharp knife. Put 2 tbsp olive oil in a bowl with the thyme, 2 rosemary sprigs and the garlic. Season the lamb with pepper, add to the bowl and turn to coat in the oil. Leave to marinate for 3–4 hours, then remove the lamb, saving the rosemary sprigs for the jus.

Heat the oven to 200°C/Gas 6. Heat 2 tbsp olive oil in a wide pan, add the vegetables and remaining rosemary, toss to mix and sauté for a few minutes to soften slightly, then transfer to an oiled roasting pan and roast in the oven for 15 minutes.

Meanwhile, heat a cast-iron frying pan and add 2 tbsp oil. When very hot, add the lamb, skin-side down, and sear until well browned on all sides. Add to the roasting pan and roast for about 15 minutes, then lift the meat on to a warm platter with the vegetables and rest in a warm place.

Add the sherry vinegar to the roasting pan, stirring to deglaze, then add the wine and bring to the boil. Add the reserved rosemary and simmer for 10 minutes. Skim off any fat from the jus, season and strain into a warm jug.

Cut each rump into 3 or 4 slices. Spoon the roasted vegetables on to warm plates and arrange the lamb on top. Drizzle the rosemary jus over and around the plate, and serve.

"Rump or chump of lamb is an ideal cut when you are cooking for two. If possible, buy West Country lamb, which yields good-sized rumps. These lambs are weaned naturally and then fed on grass so the flavour of the meat is superb. Lamb should be hung for 2–3 weeks to maximise the flavour. Look for meat that's dark red in colour with a matt appearance"

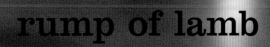

chateaubriand for two

Serves 2

500g piece fillet of beef

1 red onion, cut into thin wedges

4 garlic cloves (unpeeled)

3 tbsp olive oil

1 tbsp sherry vinegar

1 glass of red wine

sea salt and pepper

Trim the beef fillet of any fat or sinew. Wrap in cling film, twisting the ends tightly to secure, then roll the meat to even up the shape. Refrigerate for 24 hours.

Heat the oven to 200°C/Gas 6. Put the onion and garlic in a roasting pan and drizzle with 1 tbsp olive oil. Put into the oven for 5 minutes while you sear the beef.

Heat a cast-iron frying pan, and add the remaining olive oil. When hot, add the beef fillet and sear quickly on all sides over a high heat. Add the seared fillet to the roasting pan and roast for 10–15 minutes, according to how rare you like your beef. Transfer the meat and vegetables to a warm plate and rest for 15 minutes.

Meanwhile, deglaze the roasting pan with the sherry vinegar, scraping up the sediment, then pour in the wine and boil to reduce by half. Strain, season with salt and pepper to taste and keep warm. Carve the beef into thick slices and arrange on warm plates with the roasted garlic and onions. Drizzle with the jus and serve with oven chips (page 60) or flavoured mash, and a green vegetable.

calf's liver
WITH GREEN PEPPERCORN SAUCE

Serves 2

4 tbsp olive oil

2 large banana shallots, finely chopped

1 tbsp demerara sugar

1 thyme sprig, leaves stripped

1 tbsp sherry vinegar

1 tbsp green peppercorns in brine, rinsed

200g calf's liver, trimmed and cut into 1cm thick slices

sea salt

1 tbsp chopped parsley

Heat 2 tbsp olive oil in a pan and sauté the shallots for 5 minutes until softened. Add the sugar and thyme leaves and cook for 5 minutes, then add the sherry vinegar and green peppercorns.

Heat the remaining oil in a large, non-stick frying pan. Add the calf's liver slices and sauté quickly until they are browned on the outside, but still pink and juicy within, about 1–1$\frac{1}{2}$ minutes each side. Season lightly with salt.

Arrange the liver on warm plates, top with the pepper sauce and sprinkle with chopped parsley. Serve immediately.

peach melba

Pour the wine into a small pan, add 150g of the
sugar and the honey. Slowly bring to the boil, stirring
to dissolve. Lower heat, add the peaches and simmer
for 10 minutes. Leave to cool in the wine syrup.

Gently cook the raspberries in a small pan with
the remaining sugar until soft, breaking them up as
they cook. Add a little of the wine syrup to make a
sauce, then pass through a sieve to remove the seeds.

Arrange the peach halves on two plates, top
each with a scoop of ice cream, drizzle with the
raspberry sauce and serve.

Serves 2

¾ bottle dry white wine

190g caster sugar

60g thin honey

2 firm ripe peaches, halved
   and pitted

80g raspberries, plus a few
   extra to serve

4 scoops of vanilla ice
   cream

hot chocolate fondant

Serves 2

50g unsalted butter, plus extra to grease

2 tsp cocoa powder, to dust

50g good-quality bitter chocolate (minimum 70% cocoa solids),
   in pieces

1 free-range egg

1 free-range egg yolk

60g caster sugar

50g plain flour

has a divine melting texture and the liquid centre is sublime"

Heat the oven to 160°C/Gas 3. Butter two large ramekins, about 7.5cm in diameter, then dust liberally with cocoa.

Slowly melt the chocolate and butter in a small bowl set over a pan of hot water, then take off the heat and stir until smooth. Leave to cool for 10 minutes.

Using an electric whisk, whisk the whole egg, egg yolk and sugar together until pale and thick, then incorporate the chocolate mixture.

Sift the flour over the mixture and gently fold in, using a large metal spoon. Divide between the ramekins and bake for 12 minutes.

Turn the chocolate fondants out on to warmed plates and serve immediately.

salt baked pineapple

Serves 2

1 baby pineapple

about 10 cloves

2kg coarse sea salt

1–2 tbsp Chinese five-spice
  powder

1–2 egg whites, lightly
  beaten

herby mascarpone:

2–3 tbsp mascarpone

small handful of shredded
  basil

Heat the oven to 190°C/Gas 5. Stud the 'eyes' of the pineapple with cloves. Season the salt with the five-spice powder, then mix with the egg whites. Pack the salt mixture around the pineapple to cover the skin completely. Put the remaining salt into a baking tin and sit the pineapple on top.

Bake the pineapple on the lowest oven shelf for 20 minutes. Meanwhile, mix the mascarpone with the basil. Leave the baked pineapple until cool enough to handle, then crack open the salt crust and remove it.

Cut the pineapple in half and then into quarters. Carefully cut each wedge away from the skin. Serve at once, topped with a spoonful of herby mascarpone.

cooking for a
crowd

When our extended family is around, we are cooking for a crowd. I usually opt for food that can be prepared well in advance, and needs little final attention. A big casserole or pan is the key here, one that you can both cook in and take to the table. Getting everyone to the table at once can be a challenge in itself, so casual service is imperative. Catalan of cod is an impressive dish that couldn't be easier. As you lift the lid, the amazing aroma stimulates appetites. Follow with a pecan pie and everyone will be more than satisfied.

fennel soup
WITH SPICY MERGUEZ SAUSAGE

Serves 10

6 tbsp olive oil

6 fennel bulbs, trimmed and finely sliced

2 celery sticks, finely sliced

3 garlic cloves, finely chopped

2 litres light chicken stock

handful of flat-leaf parsley, stalks and leaves separated

½ tsp freshly ground coriander seeds

2 bay leaves

sea salt and pepper

410g can cannellini beans, drained

500g Merguez sausages, finely sliced

"Merguez is a French spicy beef sausage, similar to chorizo. As you pan-fry the sausage, it oozes a colourful, spicy oil – perfect to drizzle over the finished soup"

Heat 4 tbsp olive oil in a large pan. Add the fennel, celery and garlic, and sweat for 5 minutes over a medium-low heat until softened but not coloured. Add the stock, parsley stalks, ground coriander, bay leaves and seasoning. Bring to a simmer and simmer gently for 40 minutes. Discard the bay leaves and parsley stalks and let cool slightly. Chop the parsley leaves and set aside.

Whiz the soup in a blender until velvety smooth and return to the pan. Add the beans and heat through gently, stirring occasionally. Check the seasoning.

Meanwhile, heat the remaining oil in a large frying pan and fry the sausage slices for 3–4 minutes until crisp. Remove with a slotted spoon and drain on kitchen paper, reserving the oil in the pan.

Divide the sausage slices between warm soup bowls, placing them around the edge. Ladle the soup into the middle, scatter with the chopped parsley and drizzle with the reserved spicy oil. Serve immediately.

fennel soup

seafood bisque

Serves 10

3 tbsp olive oil

2 shallots, finely chopped

2 fennel bulbs, trimmed and
   finely sliced

4 celery sticks, sliced

2 carrots, chopped

2 star anise

2 tsp cayenne pepper

pinch of saffron threads

6 beef tomatoes, deseeded
   and chopped

100ml brandy

500ml white wine

3 litres fish stock

1kg fresh mussels

5 large potatoes, peeled and
   diced

sea salt and pepper

500g monkfish fillets, cut
   into chunks

500g red mullet fillets, cut
   into 3cm pieces

Heat the olive oil in a large pan. Add the shallots, fennel, celery, carrots, star anise, cayenne and a few saffron threads. Cook, stirring, over a medium heat for a few minutes.

Add the tomatoes, lower the heat and cook for 5 minutes. Add the brandy and let bubble to reduce, then pour in the wine. Cook until the liquor has reduced down to a syrupy consistency. Stir in the stock, bring to a simmer and cook gently for 1 hour.

Meanwhile, clean the mussels. Scrub the shells thoroughly in cold water and pull away the beards; discard any open mussels.

Cook the potatoes in salted water with a few saffron threads for about 10 minutes until just tender; drain.

Whiz the soup until smooth, using a blender. Pass through a fine chinois into a clean pan and set aside.

Heat a third of the remaining stock in a large pan, add the mussels, cover tightly and cook for 3–5 minutes until they open; discard any that stay closed.

Poach the monkfish and red mullet in the rest of the stock in a shallow pan for about 2–3 minutes until just cooked.

Add the potatoes to the soup and reheat, then add the fish and mussels, and check the seasoning. Ladle into warm bowls and serve with crusty bread.

catalan of cod

Heat the olive oil in a very large, wide saucepan
(that has a tight-fitting lid). Add the chorizo and
garlic, and pan-fry for 3–4 minutes. Take off the heat.

Lay the cod on the sausage and season with pepper.
Cover with the tomatoes, season again and add the
thyme and bay leaves. Pour on the wine to cover, then
top with the mussels. Cover tightly, bring to the boil,
then lower the heat. Cook for 8–10 minutes until the
mussels open; discard any that don't. Check seasoning.

Scatter over the basil and ladle into warm bowls.
Serve immediately, with the olives and eggs on the side.

Serves 10

4 tbsp olive oil

2 small chorizo sausages,
   chopped

4 garlic cloves, chopped

10 cod fillets, 150g each

sea salt and pepper

16 beef tomatoes, sliced

2 thyme sprigs

4 bay leaves

1 bottle dry white wine

1kg fresh mussels, cleaned

handful of chopped basil

5 hard-boiled eggs, quartered

250g pitted back olives

tagine of lamb

> "I love the aromatic flavours in this Moroccan style dish. Use a tagine if you happen to have one, otherwise a heavy-based pan with lid, or flame-proof casserole will do fine"

Serves 10

6 tbsp olive oil

2kg boneless lean lamb, cut into 2–3cm cubes

3 large onions, finely chopped

4 garlic cloves, chopped

3 tsp Moroccan spice

1 tsp ground cumin

2cm piece fresh root ginger, peeled and finely sliced

4 plum tomatoes, skinned, deseeded and chopped

500ml medium dry white wine

500ml light chicken stock

200g ready-to-eat dried apricots

sea salt and pepper

Heat 3 tbsp olive oil in a large pan or tagine and sauté the lamb in batches over a high heat, removing each batch with a slotted spoon and adding more oil to the pan as necessary.

Lower the heat, add the onions and cook for a few minutes to soften, then add the garlic, Moroccan spice, cumin and ginger. Cook, stirring, for a further minute, then return all the meat to the pan.

Add the tomatoes, wine and stock and bring to the boil, then lower the heat, cover and simmer gently for 2 hours.

Add the dried apricots and check the seasoning. Cook for a further 20 minutes or until the lamb is meltingly tender. Serve with steamed couscous and a green vegetable or salad.

cold roast fillet of beef

WITH WATERCRESS AND BEETROOT FONDANT

Heat the oven to 220°C/Gas 7. Trim the beef of any fat or sinew and season with pepper. Place a heavy-based frying pan over a high heat. Add the olive oil with the garlic cloves and rosemary, then add the beef fillet and sear on all sides. Transfer the meat and flavourings to a large roasting pan and roast for 15 minutes. Allow to cool.

Trim the baby beetroot tops, leaving on a little of the leafy stalks. Place on a large piece of foil in another large roasting pan and scatter with sea salt. Scrunch up the foil around the beetroot, leaving the top of the package open. Roast in the oven for 20–30 minutes.

Serves 10

1 fillet of beef, about 2kg

sea salt and pepper

4 tbsp olive oil

handful of garlic cloves
  (unpeeled)

few rosemary sprigs

large bunch of baby beetroot,
  washed

50g butter

3 bunches of watercress, trimmed

Allow the cooked beetroot to cool, then peel. (You can prepare ahead to this stage – refrigerate the beef and beetroot, but bring the meat back to room temperature before serving.)

Heat the butter in a medium pan, add the beetroot and cook gently, stirring frequently, until well glazed.

Thinly slice the beef, arrange on a large oval platter and surround with the watercress sprigs. Spoon the warm glazed beetroot over the watercress and serve immediately.

"I promise you this cold roast fillet will taste superb – as long as you've bought a good piece of beef. Superior butchers, small producers and farmers' markets are good sources of quality meat"

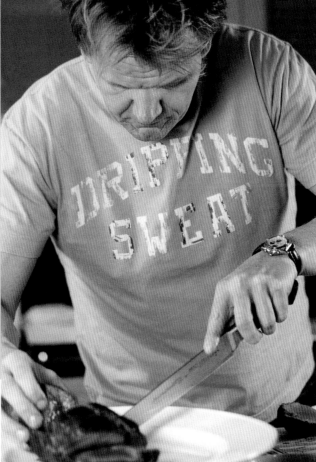

potage of ham hocks
WITH WHITE BEANS

Serves 10

4 ham hocks

1 head of celery, finely
   chopped

2 leeks, finely sliced

2 carrots, finely sliced

1 celeriac, cut into julienne

1 garlic bulb, halved
   crossways

2 handfuls of parsley, stalks
   and leaves separated

4 bay leaves

8 thyme sprigs

½ tsp freshly ground
   coriander seeds

sea salt and pepper

2 litres chicken stock

4 x 420g cans butter beans,
   drained

handful of chervil sprigs,
   chopped

A day in advance, place the ham hocks in two large saucepans and cover with cold water. Leave to soak overnight in a cool place.

The next day, discard the water and return the ham hocks to the pans. Add half the vegetables, garlic, parsley stalks, bay leaves, thyme and coriander seeds to each pan and season with pepper.

Pour half the stock into each pan and top up with water as necessary to cover the ham hocks. Bring to the boil, lower the heat and skim, then simmer for 2 hours. Allow to cool in the pans.

Lift out the ham hocks on to a board and carefully remove the skin. Discard the herbs from the broth. Strip the meat from the bone, cut into bite-sized pieces and return to the pans. Chop the parsley leaves.

Add the butter beans and bring to the boil, then lower the heat. Season to taste and simmer for about 10 minutes. Ladle into warm bowls and scatter with the chopped parsley and chervil to serve.

persian style aubergines

Serves 10

5 aubergines

200g basmati rice, rinsed

sea salt and pepper

2 onions, finely diced

400g cherry tomatoes, halved

120g pine nuts, lightly toasted

1 tsp ground allspice

2 tbsp chopped flat-leaf parsley

8 tbsp olive oil

Halve the aubergines lengthways, then score the flesh on the diagonal with a sharp knife, taking care to avoid piercing the base or edges. Carefully scoop out the aubergine flesh with a spoon, leaving 1cm shells. (Set aside half of the flesh; keep the rest for another recipe.)

Cook the rice in boiling salted water for about 15 minutes until just tender, then drain and rinse under cold water. Drain well and tip into a large bowl.

Dice the reserved aubergine flesh and add to the rice with the onions, cherry tomatoes, pine nuts, allspice and parsley. Toss together and season with salt and pepper to taste. Drizzle in half of the olive oil and mix well. Cover and leave the stuffing to stand at room temperature for 30 minutes to allow the flavours to blend. Heat the oven to 190°C/Gas 5.

Divide the stuffing between the aubergine shells, piling it quite high in the middle. Drizzle with the remaining olive oil and bake for 12–14 minutes or until the aubergine skins are glossy and the filling is beginning to brown. Serve hot.

boulangère potatoes

Serves 10

knob of butter to grease

8 tbsp olive oil

4 large shallots, finely
  chopped

8 large potatoes, such as
  King Edward or Desirée,
  peeled

sea salt and pepper

800ml chicken stock

10 smoked bacon rashers,
  (ideally Alsace), derinded

Heat the oven to 190°C/Gas 5. Cut ten 20cm squares of baking parchment and lightly butter the middle of each square.

Heat half the olive oil in a medium frying pan, add the shallots and cook over a low heat for about 12 minutes until softened.

Finely slice the potatoes. Arrange half the potato slices overlapping to roughly cover a 10cm circle in the middle of each parchment square. Scatter the shallots evenly over the potato rounds and season with salt and pepper. Cover with the rest of the potato, overlapping the slices again.

Transfer the parcels to a shallow baking tray, bringing the paper up and around the potato but leaving the top open.

Bring the stock to the boil and carefully pour around the potato. Brush the top of the potato cakes with the remaining olive oil. Bake for 25–35 minutes until the potatoes are tender and golden brown on top.

Meanwhile, lay the bacon rashers side by side on a baking sheet and place another baking sheet on top to keep them flat. Cook in the oven (on a shelf above the potato cakes) for the last 10 minutes, until crisp. Drain on kitchen paper.

Top each potato cake with a slice of crispy bacon and serve, in the paper.

pecan pie
WITH A CINNAMON CRUST

Serves 10

300g cinnamon shortcrust
  pastry (see right)

Filling:

2 sweet potatoes, scrubbed

50g light brown sugar

50g caster sugar

½ free-range egg, beaten

25ml double cream

25g soft unsalted butter

1 tsp vanilla extract

¼ tsp ground cinnamon

pinch of ground mixed spice

pinch of freshly grated
  nutmeg

Topping:

150g brown sugar

75ml golden syrup

1½ free-range eggs,
  beaten

30g unsalted butter

2 tsp vanilla extract

pinch of ground cinnamon

250g pecan nut halves

Heat the oven to 190°C/Gas 5. Bake the sweet potatoes for 30–40 minutes or until tender when pierced with a knife.

Roll out the pastry as thinly as possible and use to line a 5cm deep, 20cm flan tin. Press well into the edges and leave the excess pastry overhanging the edge. Line with greaseproof paper and fill with dried beans or rice. Rest in the fridge for 20 minutes, then bake for 10 minutes. Allow to cool. Turn the oven down to 160°C/Gas 3.

Halve the sweet potatoes and scoop out the flesh into a food processor. Add both sugars, the egg, cream, butter, vanilla and ground spices. Process until just smooth.

Trim the pastry edge level with the top of the tin, using a sharp knife. Pour in the sweet potato filling.

For the topping, whisk the sugar, golden syrup, eggs, butter, vanilla and cinnamon together in a bowl, using an electric whisk until smooth. Spoon the mixture evenly over the filling.

Arrange the pecans on top, pressing them down slightly. Bake for 1¾ hours or until a knife inserted in the middle comes out clean. Leave to cool in the tin.

Serve cut into small wedges at room temperature, with pouring cream.

cinnamon pastry Put 300g plain flour, a pinch of salt, $\frac{1}{2}$ tsp ground cinnamon, 15g caster sugar and 150g chilled diced butter into a food processor and process briefly until the mixture resembles breadcrumbs. Add 1 small free-range egg yolk and 1–2 tsp cold water and whiz for 30 seconds. Continue to add a little water and pulse until you have a smooth dough that holds together. Transfer to a lightly floured surface and knead gently until smooth, then wrap in cling film and rest in the fridge for 30 minutes before rolling out.

whole baked apples

WITH CRANBERRIES AND SULTANAS

Serves 10

10 large Bramley apples

125g dried cranberries

125g sultanas

finely grated zest of
   2 oranges

100ml Cointreau

125g demerara sugar

125g unsalted butter

300ml double cream

Heat the oven to 200°C/Gas 6. Using an apple corer or sharp knife, carefully remove the apple cores (you'll be removing a cylinder about 2.5cm in diameter). With a sharp knife, make a light incision around the circumference of each apple (to ensure that the apple skins don't burst in the oven).

In a small bowl, mix together the cranberries, sultanas, orange zest, Cointreau and sugar.

Place the apples in an ovenproof dish and fill the cavities with the cranberry mixture. Top each with a knob of butter. Bake the apples for 35–40 minutes or until golden brown and soft in the centre.

Pour a little cream into the centre of each apple and serve immediately.

"Bramleys are my first choice here, but you could use any other good tart, cooking apple. Experiment with different fillings, adding nuts if you like. Try dried mango and pecans, or dried pineapple and macadamia nuts"

my storecupboard
and equipment

The key to a really successful professional home kitchen is good quality equipment and a well-stocked storecupboard. You don't need a lot of items, but having the necessary basic tools and small appliances is really important. Similarly, a good storecupboard with all your essential dry ingredients to hand makes cooking quicker and easier. I regard my basics – stocks, vinaigrette and stock syrup – as essential standbys too. With the best ingredients and the right equipment, it is so easy to produce quality food.

my storecupboard

Freshly ground sea salt and pepper feature throughout my recipes and I cannot stress the importance of quality enough here. A dish can be ruined if you season it with bitter-tasting salt or harsh ground pepper. For its purity, we use French sea salt made from the foam of the wave rather than the seabed. Invest in robust salt and pepper mills, and freshly grind salt and pepper as required. Buy good-quality peppercorns – white, black and green – and experiment until you find the blend that you prefer.

Spices need to be kept fresh in sealed jars away from direct light. Buy spices as and when required – their flavour will deteriorate over time. Many Asian food stores and other speciality stores sell spices by weight, so you can purchase small amounts. In the restaurants, we use the following spices on a daily basis: coriander seeds (kept in a clean mill to be freshly ground), juniper berries, star anise, curry powder, smoked paprika (the Spanish paprika is my favourite), cardamom pods, caraway seeds, ground cumin, whole cloves, nutmeg (freshly grated), mace flakes, turmeric and, last but not least, saffron. When buying saffron, look for long threads with a strong colour and don't be put off by the price – you need very little to impart colour and flavour. Don't be tempted by the less expensive powder, as it is quite inferior.

Vinegars are used to deglaze pans, as well as to flavour vinaigrettes, dressings and sauces. We use sherry vinegar, balsamic vinegar (a good aged Italian variety), white wine vinegar and Cabernet Sauvignon vinegar – a red wine variety with a good, robust flavour.

Oils need to be chosen carefully, to ensure their depth and flavour is appropriate for any given recipe. The flavour of an oil must not overpower a dish, which is why I use groundnut oil to soften the flavour of extra-virgin olive oil in my vinaigrette. I like to keep a selection of oils for different purposes, including sunflower and groundnut oil. I use extra virgin olive oil for dressings and a light olive oil for frying. Hazelnut and sesame oils lend special flavours to dressings, while a drizzle of truffle oil will elevate a sauce or soup.

Sauces and condiments are used for flavouring. The most important are soy sauce (look for a good natural fermentation), Tabasco (a traditional chilli sauce), tamarind extract (from the Indian fruit of the same name), oyster sauce (for a Chinese twist), Worcestershire sauce (the stalwart of English cookery), mustards (wholegrain, Dijon and English), and tomato ketchup...no kitchen should be without it!

Rice is an indispensable ingredient and I always have several types in stock – for different purposes. For risotto, my preference is Carnaroli, but if you can't find it then use Arborio. I also like aromatic Thai Jasmine rice and Indian basmati rice. For the occasional rice pudding, there's short-grained pudding rice. It is essential to use the correct type of rice for a recipe.

Chocolate for desserts should always be of a very good quality – Valhrona is my favourite brand. When you are buying dark chocolate, look for a minimum of 70% cocoa solids. We also use milk chocolate and white chocolate, but to a lesser extent.

Spirits and liqueurs are used to enhance the flavours of my sauces and desserts and I would advocate keeping a good brandy or Cognac, Madeira, Noilly Prat and kirsch in the kitchen. Of course, I also use red and white wine for cooking, but I'm assuming you will have some freshly opened to hand. Don't use wine that's been left in a cupboard for days – it is liable to ruin the flavour of a dish.

Other storecupboard essentials are flours (plain, strong bread, buckwheat and pasta flours), arrowroot, sugars (caster, icing, Demerara and soft brown), honey, glucose syrup, maple syrup, dried fruits and leaf gelatine. We also have jars of capers, caper berries, good anchovies and olives to hand. Some ingredients considered to be storecupboard ingredients, such as nuts, are better bought as and when you need them, because they stale relatively quickly.

basics

These few standbys will make all the difference to the flavour of a dish – fresh stocks in particular. Make up these stocks in batches and keep them in the fridge (for up to 5 days) or freezer (up to 3 months) until required.

Chicken stock

Put 1 chopped carrot, 1 chopped onion, 2 sliced celery sticks and 1 sliced leek in a large pan with 2 tbsp oil and cook over medium heat until golden. Add a sprig of thyme, 1 bay leaf, 3 peeled garlic cloves, 2 tbsp tomato purée and 2 tbsp white flour, and cook, stirring, for a few minutes. Add 1kg raw chicken bones, cover with plenty of cold water and season lightly. Bring to the boil and skim. Simmer for 1 hour and then pass through a chinois. Adjust the seasoning. Makes about 1.5 litres.

Brown chicken stock

This is used for a greater depth of flavour. Follow the above recipe, roasting the chicken bones at 200°C/Gas 6 for 20 minutes before adding them.

Fish stock

This is quick to make, using fish trimmings, or you can use crab or lobster shells. Heat 2 tbsp oil in a large pan. Add $^1/_2$ chopped onion, $^1/_2$ sliced celery stick and 1 chopped fennel slice, and cook until soft but not coloured. Add 1kg fish trimmings (white fish bones and heads), a glass of white wine and water to cover. Bring to the boil, season lightly and simmer for 20 minutes. Pass through a chinois and adjust the seasoning. Makes about 1 litre.

Classic vinaigrette

Put 100ml extra virgin olive oil, 100ml groundnut oil, 3 tbsp white wine vinegar, a squeeze of lemon (to taste), 1 tbsp water, sea salt and pepper in a bowl and whiz using a hand-held stick blender. Refrigerate until required. Shake well before use.

Stock syrup

Put 550g granulated sugar, 1 litre cold water and the grated zest of 1 lemon in a pan. Dissolve the sugar over a low heat, then boil for 5 minutes. Cool, then pour the stock syrup into a jar, seal and refrigerate (for up to 1 month) until needed.

equipment

Good quality tools in the kitchen are important to the success of your cooking. When I'm buying equipment, I am primarily choosing on the basis of practicality and purpose. Every tool or appliance in our kitchen has a role – I'm not in favour of faddy gadgets. I also look for quality, durability and overall value for money – I don't necessarily buy the most expensive. Practicality of storage and style are other essential considerations. A beautiful granite pestle and mortar, for example, can be both a feature in the kitchen and a pleasure to use.

Knives are the first item of equipment I'm generally asked about. The most important aspect is that the blade is forged all the way through the handle, and that the knife has a good balance. One of the first tricks taught at catering college is to balance a knife on the forefinger of your working hand. It should balance at the part where the blade meets the handle – this indicates that the knife will have a good chopping motion.

There are three main types of steel: French, German and Japanese, and all have pros and cons. French steels are softer, which makes them easy to sharpen but also more vulnerable to damage and wear as they age. German steels are hard and require more skill to sharpen, but once you have a good edge to the blade it will last well. Japanese steels are similarly hard, much lighter in weight (which doesn't suit everyone) and very stylish.

The choice is a personal one, but the most important thing is that a knife should feel comfortable to handle. Buy good quality knives and they should last for ages. Over the years you will collect other knives for different uses but initially I would advocate buying the following:
• a paring knife, with a 5-7cm blade
• a chopping or cook's knife, with a 20cm blade
• a cook's knife, with a flexible 15cm blade
• a serrated knife, with a 25cm blade

Other useful specialist knives include an oyster knife, which has a short blade with a protective shield, and a small turning knife that has a curved blade used to shape turned vegetables.

Knives should be kept sharp. Blunt knives are dangerous as they have a tendency to skid off the food that you are cutting and into waiting fingers. Use a hand-held steel to keep the edge of the knife sharp and periodically sharpen them properly on a whetstone. Alternatively, find a good knife sharpening service.

Pans are the next most important purchase. In the restaurants, we use a wide range of pans, each for a specific purpose. Heavy-duty, non-stick pans are serious workhorses in the kitchen and we use these for all manner of dishes, from risottos to caramelised fruits.

A good starting set is a small 2-litre pan, a medium 3 to 4-litre pan and a large 6 to 8-litre pan, all with tight-fitting lids, plus an oval casserole that can be used on top of the stove as well as in the oven. You will also need a cast-iron frying pan or other good-quality frying pan – ideally one that can be used both on the hob and in the oven, up to 200°C/Gas 6.

Good pans should last a lifetime of cooking and come with a long warranty. The construction of the pan is the key here. Choose a heavy pan that has a good conductive base, such as copper or aluminium, with a stainless steel inner lining. Look for handles that are long and heatproof, well angled, and secured with stainless steel rivets.

Other pans I use regularly include a sautier – a saucepan with sloping sides – perfect for reducing stocks and sauces, and a pan that resembles a cappuccino cup, which is ideal for sauces that have butter or other ingredients whisked in. I'm particularly fond of my set of copper pans, which perform well and look attractive.

While vegetables and fruits can be sliced thinly with a knife, there are few chefs with the dexterity to slice with the precision and speed of the **mandolin**. We use this tool on a daily basis. You can buy stainless steel, wood or plastic mandolins and they vary in quality, the most important element being the sharpness of the blade. I am very fond of the Japanese mandolin, which has a plastic casing and isn't at all expensive.

The **chinois** is in constant use in my kitchen for straining stocks, sauces, etc. It is a strong conical sieve, perforated with small holes or made of mesh, available in various sizes. Look for a good-quality stainless steel chinois, with a long handle and a small balancing hook on the opposite side so that it can be balanced over a deep bowl or pan.

The **mouli** is another valuable straining tool, used for smooth pomme purée, soups and sauces. Made from stainless steel, the mouli comes with 2 or 3 perforated discs with different-sized holes for different uses. The mouli works by turning a handle attached to a semi-circular blade that forces the food through the perforated discs.

Another key tool is the **kitchen blowtorch** used for caramelising sugar, as for a crème brûlée, and also unmoulding frozen desserts. Apply the blowtorch to the outside of a ring mould and a dessert will be unmoulded effortlessly.

Essential small tools I wouldn't be without are: a **swivel vegetable peeler**, a **zester** (for finely paring strips of zest from citrus fruit), **stainless steel cutters** (for pastry and biscuits), at least two good **pastry brushes** (one for oiling, one for egg glazing) and strong **tweezers** (for removing the odd bone from fish, or a stray quill on a game bird).

For precision and accuracy, I would advocate a set of **digital scales**, which are easy to use and allow you to weigh ingredients directly in a bowl or pan. And I suggest you have at least two calibrated measuring jugs (in different sizes). You'll also need a **sugar thermometer** (for sugar syrups and caramel) and an **oven thermometer** to keep a check on your oven.

A good **food processor** is essential and I suggest you buy a powerful model with a magnetic drive belt situated directly beneath the bowl. I mainly use the processor for pastry and pasta dough.

A powerful **free-standing blender** is the key to velvety soups, fruit purées, frothy smoothies, etc. A hand-held **stick blender** is a convenient tool for soups and sauces, as it can be used directly in the pan or bowl. A strong, durable model is imperative, ideally one with at least two operating speeds.

A **hand-held electric mixer** is essential for whisking eggs for meringue, sponge mixtures, etc, though you may also want to invest in a free-standing mixer if you do a lot of baking. Other small appliances you may wish to buy are a **pasta machine**, an **electric juicer** and an **ice-cream maker**.

author's acknowledgements

Easy the food may be, but easy to work with I'm not, as everyone who knows me well will tell you. This special book wouldn't have been possible without the following people, who are very important to me: Mark Sargeant who has worked alongside me for so long, he's almost a 'mini-me', and I value his terrific support and infectious enthusiasm; Jill Mead for her brilliant photography – expecting her first baby at the time, Jill never ceased to amaze me – always calm, imaginative, a perfectionist at work; Helen Lewis for creating a whole new look that makes my food look amazing and in no way intimidating; Janet Illsley who referees my recipes and words, and puts them into a dream tone; Helen Tillott for working all hours on my recipes; James, the sous-chef at Claridges, for his dedication and help with the shoot; and, of course, Alison Cathie and Anne Furniss of Quadrille for their belief in me, and my ability to make my food accessible to all.

I'm also indebted to my PA, Lynne Brenner, who keeps me to my hectic schedule; Chris Hutcheson, my father-in-law, in charge of Ramsay Holdings, who has kept me on my toes for the last 10 years and turned me from a cook into the professional chef I am today; and last but not least, thanks to my adorable wife Tana, who is fast becoming a chef in her own right, and a big hug to the zoo – Megan, Jack, Holly and Tilly.

For their help with photography, I should also like to thank the traders of Borough Market, London; Brogdale Fruit Trust and David Pitchford of Read's Restaurant, both in Kent; Richard Barker of Fowlescombe Farm and Andrew Hendy of Ley Farm in Devon.